Praise for Publish

This book is EVERYTHING and more for anyone interested in publishing. It will not just give you tons of information (all in place!), but also fill you with courage for an exciting journey ahead.

— Sandhya Acharya, Children's Book Author

This book is a buffet of strategies to help you self-publish your stories. And more importantly, market them so readers find you. Try the strategies that fit. Skip the rest; you can always try them later!

— Rinda Beach, Children's Book Author

This book is both informative and practical for anyone stepping into the self-publishing world.

— Nicole Loy, Children's Book Author

It felt like Darcy Pattison was walking right beside me, giving advice as someone who's been through it and truly understands what it takes. That balance between motivation and real-world strategy is rare, and she pulled it off so well.

What made this book even more valuable to me is that it's written specifically for children's book authors. It makes such a difference to have advice that actually reflects the realities we face as children's authors.

— Azizi Tuere, Children's Book Author of the *Because I Am* series

This book includes great information, really comprehensive at a level that is super useful to someone navigating their way through the process for the first time.

— Laura Pepero, Children's Book Author

Publish a Kid's Book

Find Surprising Success Self-Publishing

Write a Book for Kids Series

Darcy Pattison

mims

Publish a Kid's Book: Find Surprising Success Self-Publishing

Mims House Books
1309 Broadway
Little Rock, AR 72202
USA
MimsHouseBooks.com

Publisher's Cataloging-in-Publication Data
Names: Pattison, Darcy, author.
Title: Publish a kid's book : find surprising success self-publishing / Darcy Pattison.
Description: Little Rock, AR: Mims House, 2026.
Identifiers: LCCN: 2025908521 | ISBN: 9781629443188 (paperback) | 9781629443041 (ebook)
Subjects: LCSH Self-publishing--United States. | Picture books for children--Authorship. | Children's literature--Marketing. | BISAC LANGUAGE ARTS & DISCIPLINES / Publishers & Publishing Industry | LANGUAGE ARTS & DISCIPLINES / Writing / Children's & Young Adult | LANGUAGE ARTS & DISCIPLINES / Writing / Business Aspects
Classification: LCC Z285.5 .P38 2025 | DDC 070.5/93--dc23

To self-publishers, the unsung heroes,
who inject vitality, diversity, and innovation
into children's literature.

Contents

Part Four
The Book - Formats, Printing and Selling

Part Five
Marketing Pre-Publication

Part Six
Marketing during Launch

Part Seven
Marketing Post-Publication

Part Eight
Educate and Entertain

Part Nine
Moving Forward

Write a Book for Kids Series

"Look, Mom, a skwy-skwayper."

My two-year-old daughter was showing off her vocabulary. Where had she learned about skyscrapers, triangles, and newts? From children's books.

I raised four children to become readers, and in the process, I fell in love with children's literature. For years, I have studied and written, written and taught about how to write children's books. In many ways, it's the same as any lesson on writing. Good literature is good literature, regardless of the age of the audience. In the *Write a Book for Kids Series*, I'm teaching how to write good literature, and how to bring it to market and find the right readers. Sometimes, there are special notes about writing for different ages. For example, the developmental growth of a sense of humor affects how you write humor for kids. But by and large, these are books about writing great stories.

The books in the series can be read in any order, depending on your needs.

- *Write a Kid's Picture Book: Create Heartfelt Stories* will help you with the short, 32-page picture books for the 0-10 year-old audience.

- *Start a Kid's Novel: Develop Story Ideas for Children's Chapter Books* helps you take a story idea and develop it into a full novel.
- *Writing a Novel for Kids: Prompts to Create Fun, Heartwarming Chapter Books* is about the process of writing going from a discussion of titles and subtitles, to a deeper look at character, plot, and subplots.
- *Tell Better Stories for Kids: Revise Your Chapter Book* helps you revise novels intended for 7-14 year olds. It helps you transform your novel from good to great.
- *Publish a Kid's Book: Find Surprising Success Self-Publishing* is meant to help you bring books to market yourself.

Pick up the books that you need when you need them.

British writer Walter de la Mare said, "I know well that only the rarest kind of best can be good enough for the young."

These books are in hopes that we will produce '...only the rarest kind of best...' for the kids who read our books.

Thanks to all the kids who have ever let me share a story with you. You have enriched my life with your enthusiasm and joy in a story well told.

Darcy Pattison
Mims House Books

Write a Book for Kids Series

Write a Kid's Picture Book: Create Heartfelt Stories

Start a Kid's Novel: Develop Story Ideas for Children's Chapter Books

Write a Book for Kids Series

Writing a Novel for Kids: Prompts to Create Fun, Heartwarming Chapter Books

Tell Better Stories for Kids: Revise Your Chapter Books

Publish a Kid's Book: Find Surprising Success Self-Publishing

Write a Book for Kids

Learn About the Series

Part One

Building Your Creative & Entrepreneurial Life

You're here because you used your creativity to write a children's book. Now, you want to be creative in a new way and bring your book to market yourself.

Hurrah! You may think you need a business book. Instead this book is about your creativity smashing headlong into the business world, and how to maintain that creativity and excitement while learning to make a profit.

Come. Learn about yourself and your creative work.

Darcy Pattison

Chapter 1
Discovery: Get Ready to Meet Yourself

You want to publish your children's stories because you want a book that you can hand to a child. That is, indeed, the subject of this book, but maybe not in the way you think. Because this book is about our journey with literature in a more intimate and in-depth way than most people will ever experience. From start to finish, idea to hardcover book, or inspiration to ebook—what is it like to be an indie publisher?

My experience is with children's picture books and chapter books, as I follow my passions and my whys. Yours may be YA thrillers, middle grade mysteries, preschool ABCs, or short-chapter Greek myths. As self-publishers, we face the same creativity problems.

For the everyday stuff—the how-tos—read my blog at *IndieKids-Books.com*. I'm in the trenches working and publishing children's books, so every question you have, I've had. I've applied problem-solving skills, failed, tried again, and again, and finally found solutions. On my blog, I provide both free and paid content about the technical how-tos and the business ideas that you're struggling with.

One reason for placing the how-tos on a blog is the volatile nature of business, with its constant changes. If I recommended that you develop a Facebook account, the platform's rules, culture, and effectiveness could change overnight. Keeping such a book updated would be impossible.

Instead, in this book, I want to focus on you and how the act of self-publishing will affect you.

Let Me Introduce You—to You!

You're on a journey toward a better you. While this may seem a strange comment for a book about self-publishing children's books, I assure you, it's true.

So you want to self-publish a book. Great.

But why?

All questions and answers about the self-publishing process come back to this basic question: Who are you and why do you want to self-publish a book right now?

The most important part of self-publishing is "self."

It means that you are a creative person embarking on a journey of creating something from nothing and bringing it to market. It's all about you. And yet...

...it's all about the audience, too. You have a story, a bit of humor, some emotions, a fascinating landscape, or a character who keeps talking to you, AND you want to bring that to a reader. Self-publishing is about you crafting a story that connects to another human.

And throughout the process, you're on a journey toward a better you!

When you learn to write for a particular audience, you step into their world.

When you learn to empathize with characters in your story, you learn afresh the raw power of words, actions, and feelings.

When you learn to bring your books to market yourself, you challenge yourself in new ways. You stretch and grow as an entrepreneur, becoming a stronger person.

This book will encourage you on that journey through the ups and downs. Because the ups are spectacular, and the downs are so lonely, so soul-sucking.

Self-publishing isn't something to undertake lightly because you'll be coming face-to-face with yourself.

Why Am I the Right/Write Person to Tell this Story?

Why self-publish? Let me tell you my answers in hopes it will help you find yours.

I self-publish children's books because I want to be creative in this particular way. I want to write for children, develop full-color picture books, and bring them to the child reader and the adults in their lives. The creativity of this type of publishing fulfills me in unexpected and delightful ways.

There are at least four ways to explain why I'm a writer of children's books.

Love of Literature

I'm the fifth out of seven children, but the first to graduate from college.

When my oldest brother started college (he had to drop out later because of an illness), I was in fifth grade. His Science Fiction and Fantasy Literature class changed my life when he brought home *The Hobbit* by J.R.R. Tolkien and *Dune* by Frank Herbert. They were the Harry Potter books of my day, and I devoured them, becoming a life-long fan of speculative fiction. It remains steadfastly my favorite genre. Even then, at ten years old, I thought, "I'd like to be on the flip side of these books. I'd like to write the books that others read."

One day, many years later, I sat at my desk and cried and re-read

Art and Fear: Observations on the Perils (and Rewards) of Artmaking by David Bayles and Ted Orland. After a year of being strung along, my middle grade fantasy novel was rejected. No contract. No book. Devastated by disappointment, I cried. Here's the passage that sustained me:

"Your job is to learn to work on your work." (p. 5) And, later, *"Until your ship comes in, the only people who will really care about your work are those who care about you personally. Those close to you know that making the work is essential to your well-being. They will always care about your work...Yet however much they love you, it still remains as true for them as for the rest of the world: learning to make your work is not their problem."* (p. 7)

Whether or not the world cares, I need to write. It's important to me, to who I am.

But what if my job also included bringing my books to market myself?

I realized this truth: no one cares about my stories as much as I do.

Not my husband. Certainly not an agent in New York City that I'd only met once. To him, I was just a potential source of income—if everything went well. It was up to me to decide where and when my stories found their audience. Because I care more than anyone else.

It's up to you to decide where and when your stories will reach an audience. Because you care about your books more than anyone else will ever care.

Brandon Sanderson is an award-winning speculative fiction author with over 50 titles. He now hosts conventions where thousands of his fans will come to talk Story (with a capital S). From his books, fans have memorized names and events, argued over plot points, and named their children after favorite characters. They buy t-shirts, necklaces, figurines, pillows, and leather-bound collector editions. His 2022 Kickstarter for four new novels startled the publishing world by funding at $41,754,153. That's 41 million!

But still—Brandon Sanderson cares more about his stories than all of those fans put together. The author always cares more. And you have to figure out how to bring the book to market, with the help of a publisher or by yourself. How can you bring your audience to your story and your story to your audience?

A book isn't finished until there's a reader.

If no one else wants to introduce readers to my story, I can and I will.

Homeschooling Led to Writing for Children

A second reason I write for children is that I am the mother of four. I homeschooled my kids for twelve years, back when it wasn't popular. Homeschooling was my choice, not because I was stuck in the midst of a pandemic or for reasons of religious fanaticism. I wanted to be part of their early lives in an intimate way, to nourish and develop their skills and passions, and to shore up their areas of difficulty. If I could produce good readers, then they could teach themselves. They could survive a poor teacher, a badly taught lesson, or just indifference. They could find books that would be their teachers.

With a background in speech therapy, I did what I knew how to do. I did therapy with my kids, even though they didn't need it. In other words, I provided a rich educational environment full of books, arts and crafts, outdoor activities, and a grounding in the Bible (because I am a woman of faith).

When my oldest daughter was five, I wondered how to teach her to write. A guide to teaching writing said that the parent or teacher must model writing in front of the kids. I should write in front of my students so they would see it as a normal part of life. I'm very good at obeying instructions, so soon I was writing daily. At first, I carried an ink pen, so I'd remember I was a writer. One day, I stuck the ink pen in my back pocket, where it leaked and ruined my favorite jeans. It was a small cost to pay to remember that I was a writer, a person who wrote consistently.

For topics to write about, I was drawn to children's literature because I was reading splendid books to my kids. I began researching how to submit manuscripts for children's books, and so the process began. I found that the best novels of children's literature were the best stories I'd ever read. It felt like I had found a home for my writing.

Family Economics

A third reason I write for children is that my husband lost his job. It happens. But it took nine months to find a new job. I hold a Master's degree in Audiology, the study of hearing and hearing loss. Finding a job in that profession would have been easy, but we had made a commitment to having me stay home with the kids until they were older. I decided that I'd find a way to make money at home, while still taking care of the kids and their education. Writing became more than a hobby, as I thought of how to use it to earn money.

Indeed, when my last child was born, our insurance company went bankrupt. And I had to have a C-section, not a cheap normal delivery. That's when my first book sold, *The River Dragon* (Lothrop, Lee & Shepard/Harpercollins, 1990). The advance almost paid for the delivery costs. I was contributing to the family income just as I had hoped I could.

Creative Community

Finally, and perhaps the most important for the purpose of this book, I write and publish children's books because I have built a creative life around writing for children. Eight books are published with legacy publishers—HarperCollins, Philomel/Penguin, Harcourt, and Arbordale—and over 70 self-published books with Mims House, my publishing company. I have taught writing for children around the nation, and spoken at national conventions for the National Science Teaching Association, the American Library Association, the National Council of Teachers of English, and the Society of Children's Book Writers and Illustrators. I know the field of children's literature and publishing children's books. I'm steeped in it, and I live it daily. I don't have all the answers, but I have my hard-won answers.

Come on this journey of discovering your passions and finding your own answers.

• • • • • • •

ACTION: Who are you and why do you want to self-publish a book right now?

Chapter 2
Passions: The What Matters

A self-publisher uses their deep insights or new ways of thinking to speak directly to the reader's wants, needs, hopes, dreams, desires, and aspirations in life. And so, to begin this journey, you need to take a deep look at yourself.

Focus Your Writing or Publishing Career

So, what do you care about? Some writers and publishers are motivated by principles: fairness, honesty, integrity, human dignity, service, or quality. But others are motivated by social issues: women's rights, gender, poverty, unemployment, health care, violence, immigration, or race. What dominates your thoughts and discussion?

If you could leave one thing to humanity after your passing, what would it be?

- The importance of friendship
- The transformative nature of self-respect
- The importance of science observation
- The ability to laugh at yourself

- The capacity to honor the creative passion inside each person

The best stories and books come from these passions, from your heart. It's important to acknowledge them early in this process and use them to shape your publishing career.

Take a moment and think about this. Write out your passions.

Once you publish, you become known for your books.

- That science fiction writer.
- The lady who writes about cats.
- The horror writer that scares me so much I can't wait for her next book.

ACTION: What would you like to be known for? Write it down.

• • • • • • •

More than One Passion? — What's Your Arnold Schwarzenegger?

When you went through the exercise to discover your passions, did you have more than one passion that you'd like to write about?

Here's the problem: you can't do more than two things at a time. It's too much to handle, especially at first. But there are times to consider a dual focus.

Because you might choose to become... (wait for it)...Arnold Schwarzenegger. He's known for his science fiction thriller movies, especially the *Terminator* series. But he alternated science fiction with comedy such as *Kindergarten Cop*. He built his career on a dual path, humor and an action/thriller character.

I began my writing career with middle grade speculative fiction novel, *The Wayfinder*, inspired by *The Hobbit* by J.R.R. Tolkien and *Dune*, by Frank Herbert. But when I thought about Schwarzenegger's example, I realized I like nonfiction science stories, too. I started writing nonfiction for kids and that nonfiction audience has grown faster than my fiction audience. It's given me a way to build a business that prospers because it's not based on just one audience.

Be careful here. I wanted my fantasy audience to grow the biggest, but it's been the nonfiction children's picture books that took off. I'll always wonder if I had focused harder on my fiction stories if it would have taken off better. But I truly love the nonfiction side, too. If you choose to try a second genre, think first where you truly want success. Do you want to succeed overall, or do you specifically want to succeed in one of those genres? If so, focus on that genre until it succeeds, then add a second genre.

•••••••

ACTION: If you had a second choice of topics or passions, what would it be? What second thing would you like to be known for?

Chapter 3
Goals: The WHY Matters

Author Dori Hillestad Butler has always focused on the reader who is transitioning from picture books to chapter books. These readers are gaining confidence in their reading skills and becoming independent readers. Her favorite genre is mysteries. Dori's mission statement is to turn nonreaders into readers.

How have those passions played out over her career?

• *The Buddy Files: Case of the Last Boy* received a 2011 Edgar Award for the best children's mystery of the year.

• *King & Kayla and the Case of the Missing Dog Treats* was named an honoree for the 2018 Theodore Geisel Award, given to the author and illustrator of the most distinguished book for beginning readers published in English in the United States during the preceding year.

• A second book in the series, *King and Kayla and the Case of the Lost Tooth* was a Theodore Geisel Award honoree in 2019.

Butler's work has been recognized for excellence because she focused on the beginning reader and her love of mysteries. Over her career, she's worked to find topics and stories for this age group. Her writing hits the right reading level and interest level for kids in second and third grade who are moving from picture books to chapter books. For Butler, the WHY of her work has built a career with a specific audience.

Likewise, your WHY will determine your success.

WHY Determines Your Audience and the Format of Your Stories

Your WHY will also determine the audience and format of your story.

Let's say you want to help people understand how to train a dog. What's the best way to do that?

- A YouTube channel about Teaching an Old Dog New Tricks.
- A mystery movie about a dog trainer who is murdered.
- An animated mystery movie about a dog family that performs circus tricks.
- Teaching a local class of teenagers how to work with dogs.
- A romance between a Rottweiler owner and a poodle owner.
- Training police K-9 units.
- Writing a children's nonfiction book about dog tricks.
- Writing a fictional picture book about cousins who want the best dog for each family, because the first decision is choosing the right dog.
- A romance about a female dog trainer and former K-9 police officer

You have choices: platform, audience, medium, tone, fiction v. nonfiction, and so on. You could get your point across by teaching, singing, animating, a YouTube channel, or simply talking to a single child. Why are you choosing to do this in a book? Why this kind of book?

Is it the audience? Is it the topics? Is it the familiarity because you only read this type of book?

This doesn't have to be complicated. Your answer may be that you love to read, and a book is just your favorite medium. That's a good enough WHY. But you may have other WHYs, and identifying them can help answer other questions later.

If you're talented at animation, you may choose a book because it's cheaper to produce, but you're keeping in mind that it could be adapted as an animated feature later. Whatever your experience, a book may still be the best option.

• • • • • • •

ACTION: Write your answer to WHY you want to publish this book? Once you answer that and commit to it, your choices about your publishing program are suddenly easier.

Chapter 4
Creativity v. Professional Despair

W hen I decided to self-publish, it was because I was at a crossroad in my creative life. I'd sold about eight books over a decade or so to legacy (traditional) publishers including HarperCollins, Harcourt, Philomel/Penguin, and Arbordale. After a couple of years with no manuscripts being picked up by a publisher, though, I didn't know what to do next. Nothing was hitting.

I know what you're thinking. You'd tell me that I wasn't writing good books. That I wasn't writing stories that would sell in "today's crowded market."

I almost fell for that emotionally crushing line.

2022 was a good year for Mims House, my publishing company, which only produces books that I write.

- My 2001 picture book, *A Little Bit of Dinosaur* (co-written with my sister, Elleen Hutcheson), broke out on the EPIC! reading app for kids with 1.65 million reads. We expanded the idea into the *A Little Bit of Dinosaur Series*, with Books 2 and 3 released in May 2023. At the date of writing this, the series has over 6 million reads on the platform.

- Book 5 in the Another Extraordinary Animal series, *Diego, the Galapagos Giant Tortoise*, received a starred Kirkus Review.
- Book 4 of the Kittytubers Series, *Kitten Friends: Quincy's Story*, completed a small but successful Kickstarter.
- And overall, the company grossed over six figures for the second year.

Some people are taken aback that I've found success like this, but here's what I know. If a legacy publisher had published these books (and likely, they would NOT have been accepted), the books would never have been submitted for awards or reviews. They would've failed because they were never given a chance. I would have been considered a mid-list author, and my books wouldn't have been considered the lead books of the season. In the overall mix of titles, they would have been lost in the crowd.

For me, deciding to self-publish was a way to avoid creative death. Either I took my work seriously and brought it to market, or I retired. For this writer, the legacy publishing world smothered my joy and creativity.

My opinions didn't count; my projects were beneath notice; my stories were worthless.

As every writer knows, if your stories are worthless, then YOU are worthless. Or, as Scheherazade learned, if you don't have a story to tell, you die.

I had a severe case of professional despair. I almost stopped writing altogether.

Instead, I started Mims House to fight that death sentence for my creative life. Writing that sounds melodramatic. And yet, I assure you that it felt that drastic. I worked hard the first couple of years because I knew I was fighting for my creative life. I still fight vigorously for my creative life.

It took me eight years to get to a position of $100K/year income, and that's one of the most discouraging things about self-publishing. Like any other start-up business, you must toil in the beginning to get attention for your books. Most businesses in the United States fail in the first three years. To succeed, you need to find ways to sell books early and to build upon early successes. I was lucky enough to self-publish a timely education book about the Common Core education standards that funded some of my early work.

In the last decade, I've learned to respect my opinion again. Certainly, I've had books that sell poorly. But I've also published books I love which have found readers, who tell others about the stories, and the readership grows. Every day is challenging and fun as I problem-solve the question of how to write, edit, publish, and market a great book.

The answers to various publishing questions are complex. I compare it to the process of finding and working with a talented illustrator on a project. First, I browse through myriads of portfolios to find something that fits my vision for a story. I must put together a brief that explains the project and expectations and negotiate a price that fits my budget. Then, I have to figure out how to write a reasonable contract, send it to the illustrator, get it signed, and pay the illustrator. Directing the project means setting deadlines, giving feedback on sketches and first images, and finally taking delivery of final art. That leads to layout and design of the actual book and production of the files needed to send to the printer. It's a blend of technical, financial, legal, and creative answers.

Self-publishing has actually expanded my creativity in ways I never expected. I now start with an idea, produce a finished book, and then make sure it finds its readers. The entire process is fascinating and absorbing. Self-publishing is a happy place for me because I've never been so creative. Self-publishing is a permanent cure for professional despair.

My advice is to choose a creative life. Stop placing all the power in the hands of others and start trusting your own creative decisions. Try, fail, and try again.

Let's think about other creative pursuits, such as painting. When an artist paints a landscape, would they allow someone to tell them things like this?

The color palette is too light. Make it a monochromatic green.

Don't include that tree.

The mountain should be higher up so the composition works better.

Um. No.

Unless the art is a commission piece, the answer is no. When the artist accepts money in return for a specific piece, that's different.

An artist can choose to pay attention to their own creative muse or to commercial concerns of what is currently selling well. Master artists such as Picasso never gave in to the commercial impulse, following his own passions instead.

That's where we stand as self-publishers. If we want a financial reward, we "write to market," that is, we consider what we can easily sell. If we write a passion project, we trust our inner muse. We can choose when to follow passion or cash. And the answer can change for each project.

Of course, there are consequences! If you follow passion, you may starve—in the short run. Accepted art styles are inevitably several years behind the avant-garde artists. But following your passion may ensure a legacy unthinkable any other way.

Mims House Awards

My legacy has grown exponentially with my self-publishing. I had eight books published with legacy publishers before I established Mims House. With Mims House, I have published over 70 books: 4 starred reviews, 4 NSTA Outstanding Science Trade Books, 2 Junior Library Guild books, 5 Eureka! Nonfiction Honor Books (CA Reading Assn.), a NSSTA Notable Social Studies Book, an NSTA

Best STEM Book, and several state or local awards. I am building a bibliography of work only available through this business method.

Man your keyboard! Fight for your creative life!

And while we're at it, let's build a successful publishing company. Because we can.

• • • • • • •

ACTION: Do you trust your creative instincts? Think of times when others have suggested changes. Did the changes create a higher quality story? Or did it just make it a different story?

What are things you can do today to choose a creative life?

Chapter 5
Respect Your Own Opinion

W e've talked about the importance of being passionate about your publishing program. But you must be <u>really</u> passionate! Why?

Because not everyone will agree with you. What will you do when someone objects or complains about your book? Will you stand firm?

An editor once told me that in the publishing industry you live or die by your opinion. When you publish a book that you passionately love, will it sell or not? You'll find out! Your success is directly tied to your opinions.

The Spidernaut Test

My nonfiction children's picture book, *Nefertiti, the Spidernaut*, tested my faith in my opinions.

In the summer of 2014, I heard a radio program that interviewed U.S. Navy Caption Suni Williams, a female astronaut who had spent time on the International Space Station (ISS). One tiny part of her duties was caring for a live spider experiment. The spider was a jumping spider named Nefertiti. Most spiders spin a web and sit back to wait passively for food to fly by. Jumping spiders, by contrast, actively hunt. They jump to catch prey such as a fruit fly or cricket.

But on the ISS, if a spider jumped, what would happen?

It would float away.

The hypothesis was that the spider would not be able to adapt to the microgravity of the ISS and would die of starvation.

It happened that the company that prepares all live animal experiments on the ISS was in Boulder, CO. My husband and I were going a month later to Denver to visit my daughter. I called and made an appointment with the ISS scientist. Her cooperation was amazing, which allowed me to write the story. Later, I found a great illustrator, and the book was off and running.

As usual, I sent the book off in the summer of 2016 for review and was stunned by the School Library Journal (SLJ) review. They trashed the book; I've never seen a review so bad.

It read, "VERDICT: *Skip this bland treatment and share the news clippings instead.*" [1]

I was devastated.

But I didn't panic. By then, I had two National Science Teaching Association (NSTA) Outstanding Science Trade Books, one from a legacy publisher and one from Mims House. Reviews are meant to start a conversation about a book, and I knew the conversation wasn't over.

I waited.

With relief, I learned that *Nefertiti, the Spidernaut* was named a 2017 NSTA Outstanding Science Trade Book. My audience, the science teachers, loved it! Since then, it has sold thousands of copies, one of my best-selling books.

So, I ask you. Is it a good book or a bad book? The SLJ reviewer didn't like it at all. The science teacher's committee liked it so much that it was recognized as a Judge's Choice.

All I can say is that in this business, you live or die by your opinion.

And I'm pretty opinionated. More than that, I finally respect my opinion.

Respect Makes Competition Comfortable

A couple of years after that, I was on the SCBWI (Society of Children's Bookwriters and Illustrators) BlueBoards, a discussion board for SCBWI members to talk about writing and publishing children's books, talking about the then new Spark Award for the best self-published book. I dislike that SCBWI award because of several things, but mostly because they segregate the books into legacy published and self-published. In fact, at the time, you could submit to the Spark OR the Golden Kite (the highest SCBWI award), but not both with the same book. Aggravating. Today, a self-publisher can't submit to the Golden Kite award at all. Unreasonable, in my view.

One person on the BlueBoards who approved of the award said, "Well, I don't want to compete with Mo Willems."

Mo Willems is the successful commercial author of the popular *Don't Let the Pigeon Drive the Bus* series.

Well, I do want to compete with him. While I respect his art, I respect my art just as much. I don't want to bring my books to market if I'm not aiming for excellence. I want to compete with the best of the best. Let me submit to the Golden Kite award!

Competing on the National Stage

One criticism of self-published books is that they will only reach a local audience. That doesn't have to be true. In my opinion—which I respect—my work can compete nationally and internationally.

The Caldecott-winning book, *Balloons Over Broadway*, by Melissa Sweet, tells the story of Tony Sarg, the puppeteer who built the balloons for the Macy's Thanksgiving Day parade because he saw them as upside down marionettes.

I had researched Tony Sarg before Sweet's book was published, and in fact, I went to Nantucket Island to look for primary sources. While there, I heard another author was writing about him. Of course, that was Melissa Sweet.

So, I shelved any idea of doing a story about Sarg, thinking it would never happen. But the 2016 election stirred up a discussion of fake news. Teachers and librarians were asking for non-political fake news stories.

In August 1937, word came that a sea monster had been sighted around Nantucket Island. The newspaper accounts spread rapidly across the nation and created an uproar for about two weeks. Then, the sea monster washed up on Nantucket's South Beach. It was a rubber balloon that Sarg had designed for that year's Thanksgiving Parade. All the news around the sea monster was fake news. We might discount it as a big publicity stunt, except it was more than that because all the newspapermen were in on it. When they printed the sea monster reports, they knew it was fake.

My nonfiction picture book, *The Nantucket Sea Monster: A Fake News Story* came out in Fall 2017. The book gives adults an opening to discuss issues of fake news, free press, and the U.S. Constitution's First Amendment with kids. In May 2018, the Houston Bar Association went to local schools to read this book and donated 100 books to school libraries in Houston.

The Nantucket Sea Monster was named a Junior Library Guild (JLG) selection. The JLG provides subscription services to libraries; they choose books in certain categories, which are then sent to the libraries. For publishers, it means that a book is on its way toward being profitable. The book was also named a 2018 Children's Literature Assembly (division of the National Council of Teachers of English) Notable Children's Book in Language Arts. When National Public Radio's "An American Experience" produced a documentary film on Tony Sarg, I was interviewed as an expert. [2]

In other words, the book has found success on a national level. And on an international level, a Korean publisher licensed rights for a Korean version.

Putting my books into the marketplace means others learn to respect my opinion and my work, too.

Passion for a Lifetime

When you publish a book, you will talk about it for a long time. As we'll discuss in more detail later, a book's copyright is for your lifetime, plus seventy years. Your great-grandchildren may talk about the book—and make a profit from it.

Five years after it's published, you'll still be setting up advertising for it.

Ten years after it's published, you may sign a licensing deal.

Fifty years after it's published, you may sign a movie deal.

Don't believe it?

In 2023, Judy Blume's middle grade chapter book *Are You There, God? It's Me, Margaret* was made into a movie—fifty years after its original publication.

Of course, not all books find such longevity and such passionate readers.

I choose to write and bring to market books that I'm passionate about, working as hard as I can for quality. My publishing program keeps in mind the long game. I want to produce classics that stand the test of time.

Now, that is respect for my opinion.

• • • • • • •

ACTION: What kind of books do you want to produce?

Chapter 6
From Fear to Confidence

W hen you self-publish, the only path to confidence is strewn with missteps, mistakes, retreats, and failure. Along the path, though, are also glimmers of hope, fantastic sentences, and rowdy characters, and small successes that steadily grow.

Buy 1000 ISBNs; Yet Study Every Crossroads

When I finally decided to self-publish, I went all in and bought 1000 ISBNs from Bowker.com, the exclusive U.S. company that handles ISBNs. When you order a book online or at a bookstore, everything is tied to the ISBN, the International Standard Book Number. An ISBN is given to a certain title in a certain format, so that the book can be identified easily. That is, the hardcover, paperback, ebook, and audiobook versions of a book each need their own ISBN number. The ISBN is part of the overall metadata for each title and format.

Currently, one ISBN costs $125; 100 ISBNs cost $575; and 1000 ISBNs cost $1500. But I bought it on a special sale, 1000 ISBNs for $850. Only $0.85/ISBN. What a deal!

Even at that bargain price, though, 1000 ISBNs represented a line in the sand. I went to a retreat about self-publishing and came home determined to give it a real trial. The first step, in my eyes, was to set up my company and buy 1000 ISBNs. After those drastic steps, there was no going back.

I was going to publish so many books that eventually I'd need another 1000 ISBNs.

And yet, every story is another decision point. At first, the pull back to working with a second-party legacy publisher is strong. Legacy publishers still hold sway in much of the book industry and some still believe that any other path besides legacy publishing will result in inferior quality. A library full of successful books seems to be overwhelming evidence against indie publishing. Your successes with bringing a book to market seem miniscule.

Let me strongly say: there are no rights and wrongs in the publishing decisions you make. If you decide to self-publish one book and then return to second-party publishing, it's okay. If one book is self-published, and the next is published with a second party—it's fine.

But if you keep choosing self-publishing, you'll eventually see successes pile up. The choice to bring books to market yourself will become the default. To reap the long-term benefits of self-publishing, you need to come to the place where this business choice is your default and you can't imagine going back to the other world except for unusual projects.

Make no mistake. The business model used for publishing no longer says anything about quality. Writers can and do write fabulous stories without a developmental editor's input. We can easily hire freelance copyeditors and designers when needed. Today's print-on-demand printers can now (almost) rival offset printing for quality.

Our fears can be overwhelming at first, but with each book, confidence will grow. Confidence in your voice and vision for storytelling, confidence in your skills in book production, confidence in your book marketing skills.

I Have Done Legacy Contracts for Unique Books

While my default process is now self-publishing, I have signed a couple of contracts with second-party publishers.

First, I did an Arkansas book. The University of Arkansas Press asked if I'd be interested in writing a book about the Crystal Bridges Museum of American Art in Bentonville, Arkansas. The museum was founded by Alice Walton, of the Walton family who founded Walmart. About 20 years ago, on a Good Friday, a stray Jack Russell terrier puppy wandered up to Alice. She adopted him and named him Good Friday Walton, aka Friday. When Alice was working on setting up the art museum, she often went to the offices on Tuesday, when the museum was closed to the public. And she often took Friday with her.

Soon, the staff started joking, "Friday comes on Tuesday."

I was commissioned to write a children's picture book that featured Friday as the main character, was set at the Crystal Bridges Museum, and included some pieces of art from the museum's collection. The title, of course, would be *Friday Comes on Tuesday.*"

The museum curators strolled the galleries with the illustrator and me to help us choose appropriate pieces of art to include in the book. We included, among others, Norman Rockwell's "Rosie the Riveter," Maxfield Parrish's "The Lantern Bearers," Frederic Remington's "Cowboy's Lullaby," Gilbert Stuart's "George Washington" portrait, and Mary Cassatt's "The Reader." Crystal Bridges handled all the permissions to adapt the works for this picture book.

Friday Comes on Tuesday was an unusual and exciting book. We had unprecedented access to the best of American art to include in a children's picture book. In addition, it was an Arkansas book: an Arkansas iconic museum, an Arkansas illustrator, and an Arkansas author.

Yes, the contract was a legacy contract, but I accepted that for such a unique book.

I also work sometimes with a small Christian publisher,

Dayspring Books, a subsidiary of Hallmark. They are also an Arkansas company, which appeals to me. Dayspring has published my pop-up books, *This Little Light of Mine, He's Got the Whole World in His Hands,* and *Jesus Loves Me.* Pop-up books require special designs, and must be offset printed and assembled. The format is outside what I can easily do with print-on-demand. This is a unique type of book and it makes sense to work with Dayspring on these.

My Default - MimsHouseBooks.com

When I write a book, my default is to publish it through Mims-HouseBooks.com. I'm running about five books per year, and have published about 70 books. I'm delighted to be building my intellectual property portfolio with children's books.

Moving from Fear to Confidence

Let's talk about some ways to move from fear to confidence.

Publish. The fundamental way to gain confidence is to practice, which means you must publish books. Not just one. Multiple books. Each book teaches you something about your process, and as you work through the process again and again, the process is refined and becomes one of your major strengths. Formatting becomes automatic. Marketing falls into rhythms.

After 40+ picture books, I know how to handle the images, how to position text, and how to best work with text and images together. The experience of various books has taught me the variables and how to deal with them.

Be brave. The only way through the difficulties of the first book is to simply face them. Break the tasks into small parts, and focus on getting the small things done. Celebrate every small success. Get through the process however you can. Then, repeat.

No book is perfect. No book is ever perfect, because I'm a one-person company. I have blind spots and quirks that mean mistakes happen. I just shrug, fix it, and move on. Harping on my mistakes doesn't help, though I try not to make the same mistake again. Beating yourself up over mistakes does no good! Just move on.

Do not disqualify yourself. Boldly go where you need to go. Don't disqualify yourself because you choose a different business plan; make them disqualify you instead.

• • • • • • •

ACTION: What is your default for publishing your next book? Take time to think about the reasons for that decision. When would you decide on independently publishing? When would you go with a third-party publisher?

Chapter 7
Success! Um, What Do You Mean?

B efore we move on, you need to think about one more thing. What does success mean to you?

- A hug from your granddaughter after you read the book with her.
- 1 million books sold.
- Earning a net (free and clear) of $1,000/month. Or six figures/year.
- Winning a state book award.
- Getting a book into a Scholastic Book Fair flyer.
- Publishing 100 books in ten years.
- Seeing a child laugh when they read your book.
- A series of books that help kids find safety in today's society.
- A backlist of at least ten books that make readers laugh.

If you only want a family book for your granddaughter, you probably shouldn't spend $5,000 on illustrations! Maybe you want your granddaughter's art in the book.

However, if success means you earn $1,000/month, your picture book budgeting will need to include high-quality illustrations or the books probably won't sell. You'll also need a budget for publicity and promotions.

When you think about publishing a book, how will you measure success? The answer to this question will rule much of how you actually publish your book. We've talked about who you are and why you want to publish a children's book, and asked you to specifically think about your audience. This time, I'm asking you to look into the future and imagine your publishing company ten or twenty years from now. What will success look like?

Great! Now that you know what you're aiming for, the decisions you make about story, illustrations, printing, distribution, and marketing will be easier.

Growth

Your answers will change and develop as you start and continue your publishing program. If your initial goal is $1,000/month, as soon as you reach that, you'll want to earn $5,000/month. Of course!

That doesn't invalidate this early consideration of your goals. It's good to start with your NOW and decide what success looks like. It helps you decide and gives you solid goals.

•••••••

ACTION: Write a paragraph about what success means to you at this stage of your career.

Chapter 8
Patience

I feel that I must add this one last character quality before we move on: patience.

When I started publishing children's books, I wanted success. Like, yesterday! I wanted immediate success with financial rewards and literary accolades.

It doesn't happen like that. Instead, waiting is a common occurrence.

- Writers wait for readers to give them feedback.
- Illustrators take their sweet time in producing art—duh!
- The copyeditor reads every word ten times—as they should.
- Waiting for reviews seems interminable.

We wait.

Patience is hard, but creating a successful children's book-publishing program takes time. And multiple books. So, multiply that waiting by 20 or 30 or 40 books.

Working with Professionals

When you're working with professionals—illustrator, narrator, copy-editor, editor, and so on—set up a reasonable timeline for their work. Competent work sometimes is slow. I try to build into contracts a mutually acceptable timeline so I know when certain tasks are due. Setting up expectations helps me deal with my impatience. And when they are late—time to give them grace, when possible.

Publication Schedule

In the legacy world, the time from signing a book license contract to the book hitting the store's shelves can be 2–5 years. Two years is fast; five years is very slow. As an indie publisher, you are nimble, able to put together a book quickly and bring it to market quickly.

Sometimes, publishing quickly is the right thing to do. Indie publishers who write for adults often publish a book a month. The rapid-release schedule allows them to maximize profits by building an audience quickly.

But sometimes, it's wiser to slow down so you can do certain tasks. Book reviews are generally a 3–4 month wait. (See more in the marketing chapter.) If the school and library market is your strength, you probably need those reviews, and it makes sense to wait for them. Or, maybe you're publishing a Fourth of July holiday book. It should probably launch a couple of months before the holiday, maybe in March. Launching it in December makes little sense.

When you look at your publication schedule, the date a certain book goes on sale, don't hurry it up. Give it the four-month lead time for reviews and choose the time of the year wisely. Don't be impatient.

Building a Career

Finally, building a career takes time.

I once went to a writing conference and each of the five speakers sold their first book to the first editor who read it. The books all found success, which is why the authors were speaking.

First book to first editor. Success.

I went home and cried.

Building a career as a children's book author rarely happens that quickly. Instead, a career is a slow build of books, each better than the last, each gathering a few new fans into your fold.

How many books do you need to be successful? There's no way to predict. (And it does depend on your definition of success in the last chapter.) But I can confidently say that it usually takes more than one.

With over 70 books in print, my perspective has changed. I know that not every book is a best seller—even if I think it should be. And the best sellers are always a surprise. Across my titles, one of the all-time best sellers is *CLANG! Ernst Chladni's Sound Experiments*. It's the story of German scientist Ernst Chladni going to the court of Emperor Napoleon to entertain with Chladni's sound experiments. After the evening show, Napoleon funds his work and the Father of Acoustics writes his seminal text in French instead of German. A NSTA Outstanding Science Trade Book, it hits the right notes (ha!) because according to the NextGen Science Standards, every second-grade class is supposed to teach about sound waves. Teachers don't just want my book; they need *CLANG!* to effectively teach 8- to 9-year-old kids about sound waves.

The successes and failures are always a surprise.

But after 70 books, there are a handful of successful books. The Pareto principle says that 80% of your income will come from 20% of your products. Indeed, some books are more financially successful than others. I'm always surprised when a favorite book doesn't sell as well as expected. But there are also happy surprises when a passion book sells well.

Early in your career, you can't give up. It takes patience to succeed.

• • • • • • •

ACTION: As you think about publishing children's books, plan multiple books at a time. This long-term thinking will serve you well. List five books that you'd like to publish! Can you list five more? Or, is there a series of books that makes sense for your publishing program?

Part Two

Understanding Your Business

The first task is to understand your business. This is a short section, because publishing is about one thing: connecting with your audience.

That's it.

You write and they read. You find ways to put your book into the right reader's hands.

That is the business of publishing.

Chapter 9
Who is YOUR Audience?

Writing and then bringing your work to market are intertwined, yet separate skills. You write with a reader in mind, an audience. You market by focusing on those readers, your audience.

Audience is the bridge that weaves through both of them. Your skill in writing something that resonates with the reader, and your skill in putting the book in those readers' hands are like turning a page over and writing on the back of it.

Writing for kids is hard because there are are two audiences: the child and the adult who actually buys the book. The kids are easy because they love good stories. Characters, action, humor, and life will always reach a child's heart. Throw in great writing—an amazing voice, superb rhythm, repetition, and resonance—and you have a chance of being embraced for a lifetime. When you get them early, you get them for life. Think of the joy brought by your favorite books as a child. (I hope your childhood was full of books!)

One year, driving across the prairies of Kansas, my almost-grown children started talking about their favorite kids' books, and the discussion went on for several hours. My heart swelled with gratitude to the authors who gave us—my family—such a rich variety of memories. The stories enriched our family life.

I am the perfect audience for my books!

• • • • • • •

ACTION: Write a paragraph about your audience.

Chapter 10
The Alpha Generation

Today, your audience is the Alpha Generation, kids born between 2010 and 2024. And the Betas are coming! Alpha kids are second-generation digital natives, who are familiar with and love the online world. Soon, the Beta Generation will flood schools, second- or even third-generation digital natives, and also AI-natives, who have never known life without artificial intelligence. Let's take a deeper look at these kids, your readers.

Through the 2010s and early 2020s, kids have been YouTube fans. Unwrapping Legos, building Legos, cartoons, educational videos, and more—kids watch videos. But a 2022 study from London-based KidsKnowBest learned this is changing. [1]

Where Do Alpha Kids Spend Time Online—And Why Does It Matter?

The Kids Know Best study said that the most popular streaming service for kids is Netflix, followed by Disney+. However, this could change if Netflix adds advertising, with up to 25% of families surveyed saying that they would leave. A price increase could jeopardize up to 80% of the subscribers. Keeping kids on a platform is complicated.

Behind the streaming services, kids use YouTube. At least they use it up to about age 10. That's when kids start switching to TikTok, or similar services.

Book authors have known that we compete with screens for kids' time, passion, and the family's buying potential. From a marketing standpoint, this is valuable information. The middle grade audience, ages 10–14, and the YA audience, ages 13 and up, live on TikTok (or a similar program). YouTube will reach kids ages 2–10 and their parents. Marketing on YouTube and TikTok is hard, and among children's book authors, it's a tough place to compete for attention. But we need to find and interact with our audience online in the coming decade. Maybe it's time to take a class in video editing?

Do We Compete with Screens

Some people say that kids don't read ebooks, preferring paper instead.
Nonsense.

In 2020, the EPIC! reading app, which is used in 90% of U.S. schools, reported 50 million readers with over 1 billion reads.[2] One billion! Notice, though, that kids are reading books! With EPIC!, kids choose from over 40,000 books: outstanding picture books, informational books, age-appropriate joke books, chapter books, and some short novels.

The report continues:

Now, more than one million teachers use Epic to assign, track and curate reading. It's not just volume either. The company says that in 2020, individual reading time, the amount spent per student per book is up 60%.

EPIC!'s sweet spot is ages 5–8, which is why I find it fascinating that kids are moving to TikTok (or its successor) at about age 10. They've outgrown EPIC! as a reading app. I wonder if they are moving to Kindle or iBooks or other ebook readers? Or are they moving to watching videos instead of reading on screens? Do we need a dedicated Tweens and Teens reading app such as EPIC!? In other words, we need more research on how kids read digitally.

How do you see your books competing for kids' attention online? As you set up your business, how do you account for the digital natives—the Alpha generation—that make up most of your audience?

Alpha generation kids (born from 2010–2025) are second-generation digital natives, and the late Alpha kids could also be considered AI-natives. They haven't known a world without digital devices that use AI. That means a discussion of whether or not they should read ebooks is rather moot. Two-year-olds know how to use smartphones and take photos. Early elementary kids know how to write a story with a large language model AI program such as ChatGPT. Instead, we should focus on how to engage the Alpha generation with great stories regardless of the platform where the story is read.

In fact, indie children's book publishers still report that paperbacks are their biggest sellers. It seems that reading ebooks takes place in school and on reading apps. Teachers will tend to use those strategies, but parents will continue to buy print books. Complicated, isn't it?

• • • • • • •

ACTION: In the last chapter, you wrote about your audience. In this chapter, we added information about the Alpha Generation. Revise your audience description by adding in Alpha characteristics. Decide if you will offer ebooks for all your books or for selected titles.

If you only choose selected titles, how will you decide when to add an ebook?

Chapter 11
Write for Kids

I often hear beginning writers say that the audience for their books is "the young-at-heart, from ages 0-99."

It's a sentimental statement, but it doesn't sell books. When your intended audience is wide, it means your writing appeals to no one. It's crucial to narrow your audience by age, interests, reading skills, and other demographics.

Demographics and Kids Books

Children's books are often divided by age levels. There's some fluidity and overlap here, but generally, these are the age levels, with the type of book and word limits. Remember that kids can read up or down across the age range. Titles can be fiction or nonfiction.

Age 0-2: Preschool or baby board books. Wordless to 100 words.

Age 2-5: Preschool picture books. Wordless to 300 words.

Age 4-8 or 5-8: Pre-K and early elementary picture books. Wordless to 1000 words, but less than 500 words preferred.

Age 7-10 or 8-10: Short chapter books. 2000-15,000 words, depending on the specific age and reading level targeted.

Age 8-12: Chapter books or middle grade novels. 20,000-60,000 words.

Age 9-14: Chapter books, middle grade, or Young Adult (on the younger side) books. 40,000-80,000 words.

Age 13 and up: Young Adult books. 50,000-150,000 words.

Types of Writing

Children's books encompass the full range of writing possible. Fiction or nonfiction, romances or mysteries, thrillers or fantasy, and so on. Kids need the full range of literature written at their grade and interest level.

Often people equate children's picture books with rhymed verse, but that's only one choice.

Let me peel back the curtain a little. When I write a children's book, I am concerned with the character, setting, plot, and theme. To do that, I consider all the literary devices available to me on both a sentence and word level: metaphor, simile, rhyme, alliteration, assonance (similar vowels), consonance (similar consonants), onomatopoeia, and so on to the more obscure tropes such as synecdoche, litotes, oxymoron, and so on.

I'm thinking about sentences: simple, compound, complex, and fragments. I'm thinking about the sound, or phonics, of each word, and the sequencing of those sounds in a sentence and passage, and how they will look on the page. For the preschool crowd, I want a compelling storytelling voice, while making the story seem to be easy to read. Parents should find it a smooth read aloud. It should pull in the kids and create an entertaining and educational experience.

Think about a story set in a zoo. Onomatopoeia might be more important than rhyming because of animal vocalizations. Using short sentences, often fragments, can establish a brisk pace that will keep kids' attention and keep the story moving.

Poetry is merely one of the writing choices available for children's books. And if it's done badly, it's a poor choice. If you don't know these poetic terms, you should take some classes before writing a children's book in rhyme: iambic, pentameter, anapest, hexameter, near rhyme, slant rhyme, anaphora, and caesura.

Writing for the Young Audience

So, how do you create a rich storytelling experience with your books?

First, you learn to write for your audience.

Let's say you have a car wreck. The way you tell your best friend about the wreck is likely to differ from how you explain it to a cop. Each person, each audience, demands a slightly distinct emphasis on details, the vocabulary used, how long the recitation takes, and where you start and end the story.

Likewise, when you tell a story for kids, the story has to fit that audience. Over the years, a specific format developed of a 32-page children's picture book. Like a sonnet, a picture book demands a certain structure to the storytelling.

Writing a Picture Book

Picture books are almost always 32 pages, because paper folds nicely in groups of eight, called a signature. Four signatures equals 32 pages, an economical size based on paper, and the needs of the printing presses. While 32 pages is the industry standard for offset presses, today's POD presses can accommodate multiples of two: 26, 28, 38, etc. However, I still use a 32-page format because if I ever have a reason to offset print, it's cheaper. For example, if I had a bulk order of 500 books, I'd try to offset print to save on print costs.

For the 32 pages, page 1 is the inside title page and is the right-hand side of the book. Pages 2 and 3, the first double-page spread, are copyright and sometimes dedication or half-title page. That means the story itself begins on pages 4–5. All the front matter is fluid and the story could even start on page 3.

That leaves pages 4–32 for the story, or fourteen double-page spreads. When I write a story, I divide it into about 14–15 sections, each section meant for a double-page spread.

Each page MUST:

1. Advance the story. Something has to happen. If the page or section is removed, the story will fall apart.
2. Provide illustration possibilities. This usually means distinctive verbs that indicate actions, which make stronger illustrations.
3. Make the reader want to turn the page. Each section of text should pull the reader forward to the next section.

If sections fail those three criteria, I revise.

How many times?

Until it's right.

When I write a picture book, I'm always thinking about how the story will play out over that 32-page format, because children know and love that format.

Vocabulary

The structure and audience demand certain vocabulary levels. If I use the word tortoise, I must also explain that a tortoise is one kind of turtle. Turtle is the big category, and a tortoise is just a subcategory of turtles. Kids need concepts like this explained, and I can't write a picture book without considering the language. However, I don't have to strictly follow a vocabulary list, as long as I make sure the story is clear and understandable, while also keeping the story as short as I can. That's usually under 500 words for fiction and under 1000 words for nonfiction.

Respect and Empathy

Another thing demanded by the audience of kids is respect. When I see a story with "little" referring to kids, I sigh.

Little Ben Goes to School

Little Marjorie Learns to Dance

Sweet Little Helen Learns to Be Kind

The term "little" isn't from a kid's point of view. They'd rarely refer to themselves as little or any terms of endearment. Can you imagine a kid saying this?

"Hello, I'm little Brucie. Nice to meet you."

Barf!

Kids dislike being talked down to, and won't read books that do this. (Unless it's satirical. For example, in *Hey, Bruce* by Ryan T. Higgins, Bruce is a T. Rex baby, who jokingly calls himself little.)

It also means you're not thinking like a kid, but an adult who sees kids as inferior. The story won't have the right tone to appeal to kids.

And this is where your journey as an author and publisher becomes interesting. You need empathy for your audience. Not superiority. You need to reenter childhood to understand and empathize with kids. They demand respect.

Takeaways v. Morals

Aesop is famous for ending his tales with, "And the moral of the story is . . ."

Many people want to teach kids a lesson with a children's book. Fine. But not if you bash them over the head with that lesson. This goes back to the respect and empathy needed to write for children.

Instead, you should SHOW, DON'T TELL. This old saying means you must figure out a way to make the ideas concrete. "Mary was mad," tells the emotion of "mad." Instead, write: "Mary stomps out of the room." The action of stomping is a concrete way of SHOWING the anger.

For a story about friendship, you could write, "Mary realized that kindness was important to friendship."

Or, you could write a story showing Mary being unkind to a stranger and then kind to a different stranger. The difference in their reactions will help Mary understand friendship. You don't have to end the storytelling with the moral, though. Children's books are stronger when the child internalizes the moral. Later, when they refer to the story, the child might say, "George shouldn't have lied. Then, he wouldn't have gotten into trouble."

I like to think about the story's takeaway, instead of a written moral. If the child takes away from the story the importance of kindness, the story has done its job. You could write out the moral at the story's end. I prefer not to do that.

Instead, I set it up so the child and adult reading to them can have a conversation.

> Adult: What do you think about this story?
>
> Child: I like how Mary was kind to the monster. Maybe I should be kinder to people, too.

When the child verbalizes the story's moral—Wow! It's stronger and more likely to stay with the child because they drew the conclusion.

It's hard to trust kids to come up with the lesson you wanted them to learn. But you need to trust the artistic process, trust the story, and ultimately trust your audience. Every child won't get it, of course, but many will.

I'm often amazed at the Academy Awards ceremony when someone receiving the award wants to preach. They've just created a stunning movie that is voted one of the best of the year. Perhaps, it's a movie about the importance of being kind to someone with dementia. And then, in the few minutes of their award speech, they want to preach the importance of, well, being kind to someone with dementia.

They are not trusting their art to do its job.

The movie they worked on has already done its job and won the award! But they don't understand that the movie has already touched people's hearts and made them think about the plight of those with dementia. Instead, they PREACH.

I don't understand it. I shake my head at their lack of understanding.

Kids don't like to be preached at either! You must trust your story to do its job, and trust the kids to understand it.

Write a great story. Show, don't tell.

Trust the story to do its job.

Trust your audience.

• • • • • • •

ACTION: Write a story two ways. First, tell the story as if an adult wants to teach a kid a lesson. Retell the same story, but from a child's point of view.

Think about the differences between the two versions.

Did the vocabulary change?

Did the story structure change?

Did you start or end at different places?

Did the "lesson" from the first version come through in the second?

Part Three
Learn Business Skills

From creative pursuits, you must now turn to business skills. But as you do this, bring your creativity with you. You'll need to draw upon your firm resolve to put books into the hands of kids. Your persistence is needed as you seek out the best business paths.

In fact, I find that learning to market my books has expanded my creativity. Running a successful publishing business is just as creative as writing the books to begin with. Come—enjoy the journey.

Chapter 12
Copyright: The Super-Power of Self-Publishing

Self-publishing's superpower is understanding copyright. Copyright means the national government is your best advocate. They protect your creative work, ensuring that you and your family will reap the benefits and profits for generations. This is called your intellectual property (IP), and you add valuable IP each time you write a new book, blog post, or create new art. In the U.S., current copyright law protects your work for your lifetime, plus seventy years. Life+70.

When you "sell" a book to a publisher, they are actually licensing your copyright. Each copyright has an unlimited number of rights based on audience, publication format, length of contract, territory, language, and more. For example, you may license paperback world rights for the lifetime of copyright (Life+70). Or, you may choose to license simplified Chinese language world rights for five years. Or, perhaps, you license your picture book—text only—to a website that teaches kids to read for five years. Anything is possible as long as the other party agrees, and you receive appropriate compensation.

You live or die by that contract where the licensed rights are spelled out. This should be a very detailed explanation of what the licensor can and can't do with your intellectual property. Details are specified, and once signed, the contract is in effect for the term agreed upon. This is a business contract; you cannot change the contract once it's signed, so be sure you understand each clause before you sign. Consult with a literary attorney if you have questions!

Most legacy publishers want a contract that extends for the lifetime of the copyright (Life+70). Does it make sense to sign a contract that remains in effect for over 100 years? (Let's assume you have 30 more years to live!) If you think about the changes in the last 100 years, we've gone from horse-drawn carriages to walking on the moon, from stenographers to voice-activated transcriptions, from black-and-white snapshots to virtual reality. What changes will come in the next 100? If you sign their contract, that publisher will exploit your IP for any or all of the new technologies, at the terms agreed upon in the contract.

If you self-publish, you reject those rights-grab contracts in favor of contracts for limited time periods and limited rights. Self-publishers like myself have rethought the wisdom of a contract from a second-party publisher. Instead, we choose to publish our way, partly so we keep control of our copyright.

Licensing Your Rights

You can license many rights: first digital rights, book club rights, audio rights, merchandise, gaming rights, textbook rights, movie rights, German audio rights, Japanese paperback rights, Swedish ebook rights, nonexclusive anthology rights, and so on. You define what a licensor can and can't do and the terms of the license, and the territory in which they can sell. The contract includes the money offered for the rights and the limits to the rights.

For example, you might license the right to display a story on a website for XXX days for $XXX. You can add in limits, too. You could include language that limits the license to a maximum of 100,000 website visitors. After that, they must pay you $xxx/1,000 viewers. It's all negotiable.

Dean Wesley Smith describes this as the magic copyright pie[1]. Some slices are large and some thin, but each license pays you something. You can divide the pie into many slices and still have licensing rights left. It's a variety of cash flow streams.

I often get asked, "Does it matter? Will you really sell other rights yourself?"

Yes. In the last five years, I've licensed these rights:

- Five-year contract for using picture book text only on a website meant to teach kids to read.
- Three-year contract to use a 700-word excerpt as part of a standardized test.
- Five-year contract for translation into simplified Chinese for a 9-book nonfiction picture book series.
- Five-year contract for the translation into Korean for a 6-book nonfiction picture book series.

I also have a three-year contract with a toy development agent to explore toy licensing possibilities for a certain book.

I've had other inquiries that didn't turn into a contract, and I expect more to come in the next 100 years. When you are passionate about a certain topic and take the time to develop books on the topic, it's important to maintain control of your books and copyright. When you treat your copyright as a valuable asset—as intellectual property —you'll learn to negotiate deals and limit the rights to only what the licensor will reasonably use.

As you study copyright, you'll understand the wisdom of the government in protecting—copyrighting—individual works. We are motivated to fight for our work because it has the potential to earn money throughout our lifetimes, and 70 years after our death. As you understand this, you'll fight for your rights.

Studying copyright may seem boring at first. But it's inspirational.

In 1972, Barbara Robinson's novel, *The Best Christmas Pageant Ever*, was published. She passed away in 2013, but in 2024, the movie adaptation debuted. Her family will continue to profit from the story and its intellectual property through 2083! That's inspirational.

For more on copyright, read *The Copyright Handbook: What Every Writer Needs to Know*, NOLO Publishing.

How to File Copyright

In the U.S., as soon as you write a story or create art, it IS copyrighted. However, if you file your copyright with the Copyright Office within thirty days of your publication, you'll have extra protections. I recommend making registration a habit.

• • • • • • •

ACTION: Set up an account at the U.S. copyright office (copyright.gov). When your book publishes, follow instructions to file the copyright. You don't need any middleman, just do it yourself.

Chapter 13
Multiple Roles

I t's important to understand your role as an indie-author-publisher (or self-publisher).

You started as an author or author/illustrator. But then you made a business decision to bring your books to market yourself. You are publishing and marketing your books yourself. It's important to keep the roles straight so you know when to make strategic decisions.

Author. You are the author! You wrote the book.

Publisher. The publisher is the person or company behind the business of bringing a book to market. Publishers are in charge of editing, layout and design, production (ebook and/or print), distribution, marketing, and copyrighting. Of course, the publisher gets the benefit of profits at the end of the year. If you self-publish, you are the publisher, along with any other roles you play.

Illustrator. You may or may not be the illustrator, the person who creates the images to go with the story. You may hire an artist. As the publisher, you can choose the illustrator, determine the method of payment, lay out the contract details, and the illustrator can choose whether they want to sign your contract and complete the required art. Depending on the contract, their art may be copyrighted in their name or in your company's name.

Art Director. When you accept the role of publisher, you also become the art director for the publishing company. You must decide about cover art or picture book art, and those decisions will affect the book's success. Or, of course, you can hire someone to act as your art director. The illustrator is not the art director, although you may allow an illustrator to creatively direct much of a project. Still, the decision about accepting the art or asking for changes (within the scope of the contract) lies with you or your designated person.

Printer. A printer is a company that uses your formatted manuscript to print and bind into a final print format. This includes offset printers and print-on-demand (POD) companies such as KDP-Amazon, Ingram, or Lulu. You pay for a service (printing and binding), and they perform that service.

POD Printer & Distributor. Some POD companies include distribution as part of their services. That is, they print the book and then package and ship it to your customer. This is sometimes called drop-shipping. But distribution can also mean the POD company makes the book available on certain platforms.

IngramSpark sends books to its sister company Ingram Wholesale, which makes your book available to all wholesale markets, both in the U.S. and internationally. KDP sends books to its sister company Amazon.com, in all countries, so your book is available in all Amazon markets. Other POD companies feed into Ingram or Amazon, or other systems. Lulu has an online bookstore, but its prices are quite high. However, Lulu has apps to connect to a Shopify, WooCommerce, or other online store platforms. When a customer orders from your Shopify store, Lulu will print, bind, and ship—usually a lucrative deal.

Full-Service Distributor. The legacy publishers deal with full-service distributors who fulfill orders on all platforms. They usually have a dedicated sales force that pitches books to bookstores, museums, gift shops, and other traditional book markets. They work with publishers who have at least $50,000–100,000 in sales per year and require a physical inventory of all titles. They also require exclusive distribution of your titles on all platforms, including ebooks and audiobooks.

Why Do Roles Matter?

I hear self-published people talking about their books in strange ways:

- "My publisher is Amazon."
- "I distribute books through Amazon."
- "My printer is Amazon."

Wrong on all points. YOU are the publisher. KDP, a division of Amazon, is a POD printer and/or distributor with whom you work. Instead, say, "My book is available on Amazon."

If you only work with KDP/Amazon, your books are only available there. If you sign up for Expanded Distribution, it just means that KDP sends the book to Ingram and takes an extra percentage to do that. Expanded Distribution is not recommended.

Be sure to express your business in accurate terms and, more importantly, understand the various roles played by those with whom you work!

Other Misconceptions

"I can't publish anywhere else because Amazon needs an exclusive." Wrong. If you KDP-POD print, then you can also do any other printing you like, whenever you like (as long as you own the ISBN. See below.) KDP has an exclusive arrangement if—and only if—you opt into the Kindle Unlimited (KU) marketing program for ebooks. There, you agree to exclusive ebook distribution in return for various marketing programs such as free days or discounted days. Notice that KU only applies to ebooks.

"Books only sell on Amazon." Wrong. Look around. You'll see books in school libraries, gift shops, grocery stores, and many more physical locations. Online, you see books at the major retailers such as Amazon, Apple, Google Books, and Kobo. But you also see them on publishers' websites, educational distributors, subscription box sets, and much more. (See more in the marketing section.) Any of those markets could carry your books. One of the biggest jobs you have is to reach out and make sure your books are available in those marketplaces. Selling on Amazon can be a set-it-up-and-forget-it method, but ignoring the book and the wider book market doesn't bring sales. Instead, I work to find new distribution markets each year.

Knowing the Publishing Roles Helps Answer Questions

Free ISBNs. Many POD companies offer free ISBNs. Should you take them up on that? Does it matter? Yes, it matters! When you register an ISBN (in the U.S.), whoever owns that ISBN becomes the publisher of record. Using a free ISBN means you are abdicating your role as publisher to the POD company. If you want to print elsewhere—publishers should be able to move to different printers for any reason—you can't because you don't own the ISBN.

Can I Publish This? You are the publisher! What do *you* think? Will you be able to market the book and make a profit? Can you reach the right audience to buy the book? Every time I publish a book, it's a calculated risk whether it will earn money. But the decision is still solely mine!

Can XXX Use My Book for ZZZ? As soon as you write a book, the U.S. Copyright Office protects it; it's recommended that you register the copyright with copyright.gov for extra legal protections, but it's not required. When you publish a book, that particular form of the story is copyrighted and cannot be used by anyone else without your permission. However, if you wrote a retelling of Goldilocks and the three bears, a folk tale long in the public domain, anyone else can write and publish another retelling of that tale. You only copyright the particular expression of a story. [1]

If someone wants to use your copyrighted story, then they should ask permission. On a case-by-case basis, you might allow someone to record it for YouTube. Or you may allow a city to use images and text to create a Book Talk trail in a local city park. But you don't have to allow any of those. It's your choice.

Objecting to the use of your book. For online activity, if you don't want your book used in a certain way, you can file a Digital Millennium Copyright Act takedown notice. Most online companies such as YouTube make this an easy process, just look for them. For print violations, send a takedown notice to the company and then follow up as needed.

Can I hire XXX to edit my book? Yes. You may hire illustrators, copyeditors, layout and design graphic artists, marketers, and more. Because you're the publisher, you're just hiring freelance help to bring the book to market. It's a good business practice to have a contract in place for freelance work, so it's helpful to identify a literary lawyer to work with when needed. It's just good business.

Do I have to pay taxes on my publishing business? Or does Amazon pay taxes for me? There are two types of taxes to remember here: income tax and sales tax. Yes, you must pay income taxes on your publishing company's profits. Depending on how your company is set up, you'll have to file and pay income tax.[2]

Amazon and other online platforms are responsible for sales tax, which varies by state and country. If you sell direct from an online store, you're also responsible for sales tax. Or, if you sell directly to a consumer, for example at a school visit or craft fair, you have to pay sales tax. Consult your accountant for more information.

• • • • • • •

ACTION: Consult with your accountant and decide if you need to pay sales tax. If so, set up an account with your state offices and plan your accounting to accommodate this.

Chapter 14
The Publishing Role

L et's look at some of the typical activities of the publisher.

Why Set Up a Children's Publishing Company?

In your role as publisher, I recommend that you set up a publishing company. When you print-on-demand (POD) with Kindle Direct Publishing (KDP), you don't have to have a company or company name. You can simply upload your book, add your name or a phrase like "Independently published," and push PUBLISH! Voila! Your book is available from Amazon. Great! Right?

No, I recommend you create a company and a company identity. Let's explore the reasons this makes sense!

Business Structures for Children's Publishing Company

The main reason for setting up a publishing company is that publishing a book is a business enterprise. You are offering a product to sell. Creating the product incurs bills, and when you sell the product, you earn income. Expense and income must be tracked. Publishing even a single book means you have become a small business. Set up your company correctly the first time around so you can track expenses, profits, pay taxes, and maybe even earn a salary. (See the chapter on An Indie Publishing Company for specifics.)

Publisher's Role - The Buck Stops Here

Beyond the business decisions setting up the publishing company, the publisher role is crucial to your success. You make all the business and creative decisions for the company. We've spent a lot of time talking about your goals, how you define success, and the type of books you hope to publish because these will form the foundation of your decisions.

It's both scary and exhilarating to become a publisher in charge of bringing books to market. Poor decisions will cause losses; wise decisions can bring profits.

The Company's Face

You will be the face of your publishing company, representing it to readers and to the business world. When you have an author photo made, it's also a photo of the publisher. You may want to write two bios for yourself, one emphasizing your role as publisher and one for your role as author.

The Company's (Only) Writer?

I don't want to publish other people. I only put up with the business activities so that I can write. Writing is my passion, not publishing. Mims House only publishes books that I author. Some authors find that they like the publishing role and add other writers to their publishing program. It's a decision you can make, if you like.

· · · · · · ·

ACTION: Decide on how you will handle your publishing role. Will you only publish books you write, or will you add other authors?

Chapter 15
Publishing Role: Your Company

A s the publisher, it's your job to set up the legal structure of your publishing company.

Why set up your own company?

I created Mims House, LLC, because it gave legitimacy to my business. For me, it was a positive step toward publishing independence. I went to a retreat about self-publishing and came home determined to give it a real trial. The first step, in my eyes, was to set up my company and buy 1,000 ISBNs. After those drastic steps, there was no going back.

It's an advantage when the company does the publishing tasks. For example, it's not an author sending books for review but rather a publishing company. The legitimacy of a publisher's business structure has smoothed over several publishing and marketing tasks. For instance, negotiations for foreign rights are easier when a publisher signs the contracts.

Legal Requirements

Here's what's crucial: create a business identity; then, according to your local and state laws, make sure you take care of sales tax, income tax, business identity, and other details required. You cannot ignore the local requirements, but usually they are easy to set up yourself or simple for most accountants.

In the U.S., there are different business structures that I'll outline here, but you should consult an accountant for individualized advice. This is just general information, is based on U.S. law, and is not legal advice.

Standard Disclaimer: I am not a lawyer or accountant. Please consult your lawyer or accountant for information about your specific needs.

Sole Proprietor. U.S. tax laws recognize a sole proprietor as a person who has a business and pays taxes through Schedule C Profit or Loss from a Business on their 1040 individual tax form. It's available to anyone.

LLC. A limited liability corporation means that the business and your personal finances are separated. You can create an LLC that is disregarded for tax purposes, or one that is considered a separate taxed organization. Either way, though, you limit your liability by creating the organization. It can be sued separately, and your personal finances are protected.

S Corp. This type of company creates an even stronger business identity, with certain requirements. For example, it must have at least one employee, so this is often created when your income is strong enough to pay yourself a salary. There are other tax benefits—consult your accountant!

C Corp. To separate a company's assets and liabilities from the owner or shareholders, set up a C Corp. This company pays corporate income taxes. It's a common business structure under U.S. law. Consult your accountant.

LLC or not? Should you incorporate or not? Your business structure is a matter to discuss with your attorney and accountant. An LLC (Limited Liability Company) limits your risk of being sued to only what the company owns. Other company structures, such as a C Corp or S Corp, offer tax benefits but also have strict requirements.

For the first few years, I created Mims House, LLC, which was a single-member LLC, disregarded for taxes. For business purposes, it was a corporation, but for tax purposes, it was "disregarded," and I filed a 1040 tax form with Schedule C for self-employed income. It was an easy solution since my income level didn't warrant anything more complicated. When my income improved, my accountant suggested I create an S Corp for tax benefits; it requires the company to pay at least one employee. That means I now pay myself a modest salary.

Other Tasks Your State or Local Government May Require

Check your state and local governments to see if any of these are required.

DBA—Doing Business As. If required, the Secretary of State for your state will have a process for registering your business structure and for establishing a DBA—Doing Business As—identity.

Business licenses: city and/or state. Many cities require businesses to hold a business license, which means you must assess and pay taxes on personal property owned by your business. Because my husband claims our office on his business, my only personal property is my computer and office furniture. It's a small annual fee to get the license and to pay taxes.

Sales Tax Accounts. Sales taxes are paid on the state level. Check your state's requirements and follow them.

Wills. Your books are intellectual property under your will. When you write your will, you should make provisions for who is in charge of your intellectual property, such as copyrights and trademarks.

Taxes. As a single-member, disregarded entity LLC for many years, I filed the 1040 and Schedule C self-employed tax forms. My accountant now provides the tax documents for my S Corp. Because I pay for professional services to marketing freelancers, illustrators, editors, and lawyers, I must provide them with 1099-NEC tax forms, which show what Mims House, LLC, paid them. This means when I sign a contract with any professional, I must obtain and keep on file a W-9 form, which asks for their social security number. Many accounting software programs, such as QuickBooks, have provisions to track and print 1099s. If not, then use a service such as Track1099.com. Always consult your accountant.

You're a Small Business - Advice

Congratulations! After you set up everything, you're a small business. And there's good news and bad news.

Good news: You're a publisher!

Bad news: In the U.S., most small businesses fail within the first 3–5 years. It often takes 7–10 years to turn a profit. The biggest problem is that they overestimate sales and underestimate the cost of operating a business. There's too much money going out and not enough coming in.

But if you're a writer, you know what to do. Put your head down and write and write and write. Isn't that what you wanted to do anyway? Then publish and publish and publish.

In the early years, hold costs down.

Do not spend anything you don't have to.

Don't buy office equipment.

Don't attend conferences.

Don't get the highest-priced illustrator.

DO make quality the highest priority—within reason. Creating a high-quality publishing program is why you started this journey, and those books will be the reason you succeed or fail. Shoot for quality in everything: writing, illustrations, copyediting, website, and so on.

Just don't spend money you don't have at first. Your goal for the first three years is to survive!

● ● ● ● ● ● ●

ACTION: Decide on your business structure and consult with professionals as needed. Obtain business licenses, set up bank accounts, and so on. Your publishing company should be legally set up.

Chapter 16
Publishing Role: Branding

P art of creating your children's publishing company is making basic decisions about the brand you will build. Publishers, this is your responsibility.

The Importance of Branding

First, and most important, what type of children's books will you publish? And who is your audience?

Mims House Books publishes fiction and nonfiction for ages 5–14, with an emphasis on science nonfiction titles.

Age Level: Children's books cover ages 0–18. That is a huge age range! You must narrow your audience somehow. MimsHouse-Books.com doesn't publish preschool books. That is an audience of parents, grandparents, early childhood centers, etc. It's a very different audience from elementary school-age children's books. Most of my books are for ages 5–10, but I do have a few outlier novels, so I include up to age 14.

Genre: Will you publish a certain genre? Do you have a passion for books about deaf children? Or will you reach for a STEM or science audience? It's crucial to define the genres you will publish, trying to stick to just one genre.

Here's where I break my own rules, and pay for it. I publish both fiction and nonfiction, but my nonfiction pays the bills. It would be easier (and probably smarter) to not publish my middle grade novels. I just accept that for marketing, I have two different audiences, and that makes my job harder.

Format: What formats will you feature? Hardcover, paperback, ebooks, audiobooks, or something else? Board books only? Mims-HouseBooks creates simultaneous hardcover, paperback, ebook, and audiobook versions. I release all formats on the same day, allowing my customers to choose books in their favorite format. For more, see the section on Printed Books and eBooks and Audiobooks.

Distribution: Will you print overseas, warehouse, and fulfill (send books to customers after an order) yourself? Or will you use POD services such as KDP, Lulu, and IngramSpark who will drop-ship after printing? How will your books go from an order to being delivered to the customer? For more, see the chapter on Printing Overseas or POD.

These are basic questions about your publishing program when you publish a children's book. But these also matter for marketing.

What Will Your Children's Publishing Company Become Known For?

One of the crucial keys to success in indie publishing is to publish a certain kind of book over and over until you become known for that. When someone is looking for a children's nonfiction science book, I hope they come to MimsHouseBooks.com first, confident that they'll find something appropriate!

• • • • • • •

ACTION: Take the time to think about what you want to be known for. Write your long-term goals here.

• • • • • • •

Once you decide your long-term goals, you can start to do branding. What's your logo, your colors, the language you use to describe your company? What's your mission statement? For example, if you publish only books about deserts, your branding colors would logically be desert colors. I publish elementary books, so I use a school bus yellow and bright blue on my website. I don't use pastels because I don't write the sentimental type of books for kids. Think about what your branding says about your books and your publishing program.

Use your name and/or logo on everything from the setup forms on your publishing program to emails, press releases, or newsletters.

It's a mistake to use "Independently Published" as your publisher's name. I think it's also a mistake to use your name, unless you plan to build your brand around your name, likeness, and imagery. I don't want to use my photo as the publisher photo, so I use the Mims House logo instead. Using your name as your publisher's name can work if you are an extrovert who enjoys putting yourself out there. But I'd rather talk about my company and my books than about myself!

With branding decisions done, create concise descriptions of your company: 50 words, 100 words, 500 words (or thereabouts). These will help you focus your publishing program and your marketing and publicity.

18 words, 116 characters: Mims House Books publishes

fiction and nonfiction for ages 5–14, with an emphasis on science or STEM nonfiction titles.

74 words, 495 characters: Mims House Books (mimshousebooks.com) has published over 70 award-winning fiction and nonfiction books for children ages 5–14, with an emphasis on science or STEM nonfiction titles. Four books have received starred PW or Kirkus reviews. Awards include five NSTA Outstanding Science Trade Books, five Eureka! Nonfiction Honor books (CA Reading Assn.), two Junior Library Guild selections, two CLA Notable Children's Books in Language Arts, a Notable Social Studies Trade Book, and a Best STEM Book.

• • • • • • •

ACTION: Take time to write your identifying descriptions to create a statement about your children's publishing company.

• • • • • • •

Where Does YOUR Audience Hang Out?

This is extremely helpful to define your publishing program, and therefore, your audience. It will help you target your publishing program effectively. What you publish and the audience you publish for defines your success. You must know this and you must stick with it. You can't change midstream or you won't have success.

Once you have clearly established your publishing program, you'll know where to find your audience! I never look at preschool opportunities. Because I rely on POD, which prices me out of bookstores, I ignore all bookstore promotions. I focus on education markets, so I'm always looking for new ways into that market. A reading app that is used in schools? I'm going to contact them immediately. I attend conventions for teachers and librarians, rather than Christmas craft markets for parents.

After you have published 10 books, 20 books, or 50 books, you should be able to look back and see that they all appeal to the same audience. Then your backlist will help sell your new titles. You'll build momentum as a publisher and find success. It will take time. One book will not bring instant success. But consistently publishing the same genre books and reaching out to the same audience can and will bring you a following.

• • • • • • •

ACTION: Based on your long term goals and your description, decide on visual branding for your company. Create a logo, decide on brand colors, and brand messaging.

Chapter 17
Publishing Role: Contracts

What contract do you need for illustrators, graphic designers, audiobook narrators, or other professionals?

When I first started Mims House, I contacted a literary lawyer, who happened to be a children's book author, for help in writing a boilerplate contract that I could customize as needed. It's a work-for-hire contract because I usually need all rights for the budget to work. That way, accounting is simplified and there's no extra reporting or communication needed for accounting. This makes sense in the beginning because sales may be slow to build, which means the illustrator wouldn't earn out the advance anyway. It's better to give them compensation up front. I'm taking on the risk of publishing and marketing, so I get the benefit when there are profits.

I issue contracts for all illustrators, audiobook narrators, cover artists, or any other professional service. Since 2000, according to the Electronic Signatures in Global and National Commerce (ESIGN) Act, digital signatures are legal and make it simpler to get contracts signed either in the U.S. or internationally. For simplicity, I use a service like SignNow.com or Docusign.com for digital signatures.

Clauses, Clauses, and Clauses

One of the important tasks of your role as publisher is to provide a contract for the illustrator, audiobook narrator, translator, or other professional. This is a legally binding agreement which lays out the roles of each party in detail. This governs all subsequent interactions. As they say, you will live or die by the contract.

But it's difficult to find anyone who will share a full sample contract. The main reason is that no one wants to be responsible for your legal issues. You should consult a literary lawyer. A boilerplate contract should run under $500. Such a template can be easily modified to suit any project and is well worth the money.

Here's a list of typical clauses in a typical contract. The list is not all-inclusive, as each contract will need some customization. But it's a place to start to understand the complexities. In the discussion below, YOU are the publisher.

Standard Disclaimer: I am not a lawyer or accountant. Please consult your lawyer or accountant for information about your specific needs.

Typical Contract Clauses for Self-Publishing

Here are typical contract clauses.

Preamble: Gives the date, the parties involved in the agreement, and the work involved. Usually, you ask for the professional's legal address.

Scope of Work, or Grant of Rights: Specifies which rights the illustrator or narrator is granting to the publisher.

Delivery of Works: Specifies dates for delivery of manuscript in various stages, and what other materials must be delivered such as photographs or permissions. Often there's another clause on Failure to Deliver.

Compensation: How much will the illustrator or narrator receive? If you intend to pay royalties, then you'd specify royalty schedules for each version of the book. If it's work-for-hire, the terms are specifically spelled out. See the list below of possible royalties to address; this is an incomplete list, but it gets you started.

Advances: Specifies the amount of an advance and delivery schedule.

Royalties: Specifies the royalty schedule for various versions of the work. Typically, there are different royalties for:

- First Serial Right: Specifies who owns these rights.
- Subsidiary Rights—Print: Specifies publisher's rights and responsibilities in licensing the work to book clubs, paperback editions, abridgments, condensations, magazines, etc.
- Subsidiary Rights—Non-Print: Specifies publisher's rights and responsibilities in licensing the work for dramatic, motion picture, television, audio, live theater, videogames, toys, calendar, etc.
- Subsidiary Rights—Electronic: Specifies publisher's rights and responsibilities in issuing and reissuing the work in an electronic format.
- Foreign Licenses: Specifies publisher's rights and responsibilities in licensing the work to foreign publishers.

Work Made For Hire: If this is work-for-hire, there's often a separate clause that specifies this agreement.

Confidentiality and Nondisclosure: Some publishers prefer to ask illustrators and narrators to sign a nondisclosure agreement.

Termination of Contract: Covers the conditions under

which the contract can be terminated, including unacceptable artwork or audio files.

Warranties and Indemnities: Publisher asks the illustrator or narrator to state that they are the creator of this work. This clause governs how lawsuits will be handled should problems arise.

Copyediting, Proofreading, and Correction of Proof: Specifies how and when copyediting, proofreading, and correction of proof will occur.

Publication: Publisher agrees to publish the work in a specified form and within certain time limits. This clause is seldom needed in a self-publishing contract.

Use of Illustrator's or Narrator's Name and Likeness: Grants and/or limits the publisher's use of illustrator's or narrator's name and likeness in publicity.

Accounting and Payments: Provides procedures and time schedules for accounting and payment of monies due under the contract.

Illustrator or Audiobook Narrator Copies: Specifies the number of free copies the illustrator or narrator will receive.

Revised Edition Clause: Specifies how the publisher will handle a revision of a work. This is especially used in updating textbooks or books which need constant updating.

Out of Print Provision: Specifies conditions under which a book is considered out of print.

Return of Manuscript: Specifies time frame and conditions for return of original manuscript.

Bankruptcy and Liquidation: Provides procedures for dealing with the publisher in case of bankruptcy or liquidation.

Suits for Infringement: Deals with dividing any money resulting from an infringement suit.

Governing Law: Specifies the state (or country) law which shall have jurisdiction in case of legal proceedings.

Successors and Assigns: Assures that if your company is bought out, the new publisher will be bound by this contract.

Waiver or Modification: Confirms that this contract is complete and binding.

Notices: Specifies that if any legal proceedings take place, there should be proper notification.

Signatures: Both parties must sign and date the document for legal purposes.

Exhibits: Sometimes the technical requirements of a project are included as an exhibit. For example, you might specify that art is provided as 300 dpi at full size, and PSD files are required for final acceptance of the art. Whatever technical requirements are needed to publish the book, you can include here.

Contracts are tricky; contracts are important. Whatever option you choose for negotiating your contract, you should continually be educating yourself about the clauses that govern your relationship with a publisher. Because everything about your book is governed by that contract. It's a legal, binding document and you shouldn't sign it without understanding it and negotiating the best terms possible.

Resources

Several author or publisher organizations offer sample contracts, often annotated with explanations of alternative phrasing for each term. As always, consult a lawyer for your individual needs.

The Authors Guild (authorsguild.org) has a model contract available online. It's for traditional publishing and therefore may be more complicated than you need. It will address things you don't need and will leave out things you do need. For example, if you prefer to use a work-for-hire contract for illustrators or narrators, this doesn't address that terminology. But it's a good place to start to understand the typical clauses in a publishing contract.

The Independent Book Publishers Association (ibpa-online.org) also offers members sample publisher or author and sample translation rights licensing agreement.

• • • • • • •

ACTION: Contact a lawyer to create a boilerplate contract for your company. Or use the samples listed above to create one. I'd still advise you to consult with a lawyer so that you don't miss anything. I know—this is one of the hardest things you'll do. But it's crucial that your contracts are set up well. Take a deep breath—and just do it.

Chapter 18
Publishing Role: Accounting

The publisher is also responsible for the finances of the publishing company.

Have you sold any writing at all, any place, any time? Yes? That means you need to know about accounting for writers. The local, state, and federal tax officials want to know how much money you made, and what you spent to make that money, and if you have anything left over as profit at the end of the day. That's accounting.

Unfortunately, I've never taken a course in accounting, so when I opened Mims House, I knew nothing. It's been painful to learn accounting, partly because I was doing everything on a tight budget which didn't stretch to hiring an accountant. My husband and I have always done our own taxes, so I thought I could do it. Besides, if I had to spend $500 on something, I wanted to contribute that to hiring a great artist for a picture book, not an accountant to take care of numbers. The choices were always easy to make. To my regret.

Accounting for Writers—Getting Started

I'm still not an expert! You should hire an accountant! Don't do what I did, but be wiser!

Standard Disclaimer: I am not a lawyer or accountant. Please consult your lawyer or accountant for information about your specific needs.

OK. If you don't believe me or if you're so broke like I was that you really can't afford an accountant, then I want to tell you my story.

At first, after investigating tons of programs, I went with the standard QuickBooks software program. It's relatively inexpensive and is widely touted as a good program. It is good—if you know what you're doing.

I'm using the terms accounting and bookkeeping separately here. Bookkeeping is the practice of recording daily transactions, either purchases or sales. Accounting is slotting all those transactions into categories. I hired an accountant friend to set up the chart of accounts—the categories—for me, and then did my own bookkeeping.

Here's the sad truth: I'd rather write a new chapter than do bookkeeping. Everything was put off and put off and put off. Twice a year, I spent a couple of agonizing weeks of bookkeeping to catch up, and I moaned during the whole process. I did it twice a year because for a couple of projects, I had a partner who needed a bi-annual accounting. Until I was required to do that for her, I flat refused to do anything. Foolish.

QuickBooks worked for a couple of years, but my accounting was badly broken. I could report my income for taxes, but everything was a mess. I also knew that my accounting wasn't set up correctly. The chart of accounts—the list of income and expense categories into which transactions are slotted—was a mess. At first, with only a few books out, I set up an account for each book. By the time I had 30 books out, that had become cumbersome, redundant, and foolish.

A New Accounting Day

For self-published or indie writers, accounting is difficult anyway. We want to write, not play with numbers. When you do look at numbers, it's complicated. Let's say that you upload ebooks directly to Apple's iBookstore. Let's assume that you sell one ebook to someone in Norway and make a profit of $0.50. You must account for that $0.50, each and every time. Multiply that times 59 countries times five different ebook platforms. It can be overwhelming.

I wanted something simple that would allow me to keep up on a daily basis. And I wanted to totally redo my chart of accounts to reflect the current status of my business. In other words, I decided on priorities for my accounting, and then went looking. I wanted to remove all the obstacles to doing good accounting, such as manually inputting transactions—something I hated to do.

After investigating, I went with Xero.com as my new accounting program. It's an online subscription, so it costs more. However, it has several advantages. First, it pulls in data from my bank, PayPal, and other financial accounts daily. In order to make that happen, I changed to an online-only banking account. I still have the local bank account from which I have to manually download transactions and then upload to Xero.com once a month. But I'm switching almost all transactions over to the online banking program so that eventually 90–95% of my transactions will be pulled daily into Xero. To deposit a check, I take a photo of the check to upload. I also chose Xero because it integrated with Shopify, the online selling platform where I host my bookstore. It also integrated with Stripe, a major platform for credit card transactions. In other words, I was also looking forward and trying to make sure I don't have to switch again anytime soon.

The biggest disadvantage is that Xero is a subscription-based service. I pay monthly. But my business is at a point where I can pay for this convenience, if it makes a difference in my bookkeeping.

And it's made a huge difference. Instead of manually adding transactions, or manually downloading or uploading from my local bank, the transactions appear like magic in Xero. My new rule is that I must check Xero daily and reconcile all outstanding transactions THAT DAY! (Well, that rule works sometimes!)

While I was at it, I consulted an accountant and redid the chart of accounts. For any given business, the chart needs to be customized. After struggling through a bad chart of accounts for a couple of years, I knew the pain points and where I wanted to change it.

Understanding Accounting

It's not enough, though, to just do bookkeeping and accounting. You need to know what it all means. Are you making a profit? How do you know?

For me, the answers have been in an amazing book, *Accounting for the Numberphobic: A Survival Guide for Small Business Owners*. I won't try to repeat what author Dawn Fotopulos says; instead, I recommend that you read her book.

· · · · · · ·

ACTIONS: Set up your accounting! Depending on your expertise, you may need to read Fotopulos's book, contact an accountant, or take a class on accounting. You can always upgrade the accounting later when your business takes off, but the basic accounting must be set up.

Chapter 19
Art Director

F ull-color children's picture books need amazing illustrations, which means you are an art director. Let's assume for the purposes of this chapter that you're a writer, and not an illustrator; you're self-publishing the book you wrote. If you're writing and publishing a middle grade novel, skim this chapter and apply it to the cover design. For those self-publishing a picture book, though, this is a crucial chapter.

To successfully hire a fantastic illustrator for your self-published children's book, you need two things: first, your vision for the book; and second, the ability to work with a talented artist. Let's look at both of these. The book's vision must be robust and definite. And yet, when you pass that vision to an artist, it must become a shared vision, probably with some compromises.

When I received the first copies of my first picture book, *The River Dragon* (Lothrop, Lee, and Shepard/Harpercollins), illustrated by Jean and Mou-Sien Tseng, I realized it was the death of one book, the book in my head, and the birth of a second book, the one I held in my hands. And the second was so much better than I could have imagined. The artist's abilities and vision far exceeded mine. I don't think in images; instead, I think in terms of image possibilities, working to provide a range of options to the illustrator. They think in images—fortunately!

Does that mean my vision was worthless? No. It means it's a starting place to create a great book because it drives my choices of illustrators.

Hiring a Fantastic Illustrator

Hiring a fantastic illustrator is one of the first "I'm shaking in my boots" moments on this journey of self-publishing. Here's the thing about searching for illustrators for your indie children's picture books: it's all about creating the best book possible. Within the bounds of your story, your creative sensibility, and your budget, how do you create the best book possible?

The problem, of course, is that you can't draw, paint, illustrate, or design a book. You only do the words. How do you work with an illustrator?

First, educate yourself about art. There's a wide range of techniques or mediums of art: woodcutting, metal etching, pencil illustration, charcoal illustration, lithography, watercolor, gouache, acrylics, collage, or pen and ink. Each of those can be hand-created or mimicked with digital media. Styles can range widely, too: realistic, concept, graphic novels, spot illustrations, double-page spreads, and more. It's important to know the range of possibilities to better visualize a completely illustrated book. Take art appreciation classes and study layout and design. The better sense you have of art, and how it can be used in a book layout, the better your decisions will become. Become an art snob! You'll be a better publisher.

The key, however, is that you know Story, with a capital S. You're a writer who has created a special story, and you've provided great prompts in the text for an illustrator. As you work through the process, concentrate on the story, not trivial details. Does the finished book create the right reader experience for your story? That's your sole criterion for judging the art.

Why I Don't Use Cheap Sites

I know. Everyone says turn to XXX (fill in the blank with your favorite site), one of the cheap places online for illustrations. This advice, to me, disrespects children's books, reducing them to "just a book for kids," as if this book doesn't need professional illustration because the audience is "just kids."

British poet Walter de la Mare said, "Only the rarest kind of best in anything can be good enough for the young."

It's a sentiment that resonates with me and reminds me to respect my readers, regardless of their age. That means I need great art.

I look for amazing art that fits my vision of the book. Much of the criticism of indie books revolves around the illustrations. Mediocre digital art in a cartoony style seems to be the first choice of many indies, much to my dismay because so often it doesn't do justice to the text. It takes time and effort to find a great illustrator. But it's time well spent. And it will pay off with better sales in the long run.

Finding Illustrators

So, let's jump into details on how to find an illustrator. I find it best to cast a wide net, certainly past your own acquaintances. Usually your neighbor who's a hobby artist will not be able to create the book of your dreams.

Behance.net is a social media platform from Adobe (the creator of professional software for artists) where illustrators worldwide post portfolios. I regularly spend time sifting through the artwork. Sometimes, I'll look for children's book artists because they'll be experienced and you'll have fewer blunders in the process. If you're not comfortable with art direction, you may want to stick to someone who's done a few books already.

Sometimes, though, I'll search Behance using a keyword related to my book, such as "spiders" or "ghosts." This widens my choices of artists. In other words, I don't care if they've published a children's book before. I'm confident that I can give enough art direction for artists to create a great book. Many of my illustrators have published their debut book with me, and gone on to more.

Behance allows you to contact the illustrator through their platform, but often, there are links to the artist's website. I usually click through because it's good to look through their entire range of art.

Professionals already working in children's books can be found through the Society of Children's Book Writers and Illustrators (SCBWI.org). They often host an online portfolio show, which is a quick way to look through a range of illustrators. Also, Reedsy.com vets illustrators (and all professionals) before they can list on the service, resulting in a higher quality list. It's probably more expensive, too, but it's quality.

Contacting Illustrators

So, you've found a great illustrator and you should contact them immediately, right? Wrong.

Let's back up to the project in question. Let's say your book is titled, **August Follies**, and is the story of a family picnic. Before you contact the illustrator, you must answer these questions.

• What kind of illustrations do you want for this book to enhance the reader's experience?
  • What style?
  • What medium?
  • How many illustrations do you need?
  • What have you allotted in your budget for an illustrator?

Beyond those questions, you need to know the specifications for the project so they can decide if the price is right for the amount of work you're asking. That means the illustrator needs to know the size book you need or the trim size, page count, and what kind of printer you'll use.

Print Specs for Illustrator

Before you contact an illustrator answer these questions.

1. How will you print the book? See the chapter on Printing Overseas or POD.
2. What trim size will work best for this project? In other words, how big, or how many inches (or cm) in width and height will the book be? Each printer will have their own standard sizes, so check before you make this decision.
3. How many pages? Standard picture books are 32 pages (See Respect Your Audience chapter for an explanation). However, with print-on-demand technology, you can go up or down—if you have a good reason.
4. Does the printer provide templates for the interior and/or cover that you can pass along to the illustrator?

Contracts for Illustrators

Next, you'll need to know what type of contract you'll offer.

Standard Disclaimer: I am not a lawyer or accountant. Please consult your lawyer or accountant for information about your specific needs.

Work for hire means the artist creates commission work specifically for this project for an agreed upon fee, and you will own all copyright to the art.

Licensing artwork usually means the artist retains copyright, and you only license the right to use the art in this project. In this case, the art may be relicensed and appear in other publications later. As part of the contract agreement, you can negotiate if the artist must wait for a time period or restrict it from certain uses, such as other children's books.

A royalty agreement means you'll be sharing the profits with the illustrator. Traditional publishers offer an advance on royalties, which means they pay the artist a certain amount upfront, and will pay no more until that amount is "earned out." Then, they specify a percentage of sale price that they'll pay. For example, an artist might receive $5000 advance, with 5% royalty for a picture book. If that book retails at $20 (to make the math easy), for each book that sells, the illustrator receives $1. The book must sell 5000 copies to "earn out" the advance. After that, the book would accumulate royalty payments that are paid out on a regular basis as specified in the contract. Some publishers offer royalty based on net proceeds instead of list price, so the book would need to sell even more copies before the advance is earned out.

A final contract agreement is a partnership, which means you and the illustrator will share any profits. Usually this is 50%–50%, but you can negotiate anything that makes sense to both parties.

As an indie publisher, how do you plan to pay the illustrator? If you consider the accounting, work for hire is the easiest, and the complexity increases with each of the other options.

The other question you must answer is how much to offer the illustrator. First, set up a budget for the book. You'll need to have an idea of other costs and how much you can afford. Keep in mind that the illustrator's time and work are valuable. I wish I could give you a figure, but it varies from $1000 to $20,000, or more. What can you afford and still make a profit? Set your budget and stick to it. There are likely a variety of illustrators available in your price range.

Illustrators and Your Production Schedule

How fast do you want the art done? It's helpful to set up a timeline for certain events in the publishing process. You'll want to include any outside deadlines or events, key dates for delivery of sketches and final art, time needed for copy edits, time needed for the book designer to complete work, time to send to review journals, and some leeway in case anything goes wrong.

Each book needs a slightly different timeline, especially if you're working with other professionals such as a book designer or copy editor.

The illustrator doesn't need to know all of that, of course, but you do because it's good practice to give them deadlines for delivery of art in a couple phases. I usually pay 25% on signing the contract, 25% on approval of sketches and 50% on delivery of final art. Sketches and final art both have deadlines.

Typical Spec Sheet for Children's Book Illustrations

After all the decisions, here's a typical spec sheet, which can be modi-fied to meet your needs. Note that many of the POD printers allow you to generate a template for InDesign (Adobe layout software) or Photoshop (Adobe photo editing software).

AUGUST FOLLIES by Jane Doe

32 page illustrated color picture book, 8.5″ × 8.5″ InDesign or Photoshop template provided that specify the final size of art with bleed. To include:

• Double-page color cover, InDesign or Photoshop template provided. This will also be used for the interior cover.

• 15 double-page spreads

• Single page illustration for page 32.

• All images must be delivered as psd files (for CMYK) at 300 dpi.

Work for hire contract, worldwide rights, with payment of $XXXX, to be paid following this schedule. 25% payment upon signing contract 25% payment upon approval of sketches, due 60 days after signing contract. 50% payment upon delivery of final art, due 180 days after sketches approved.

Now You're Ready to Contact Illustrators

Be professional. You're a book publisher with a children's book project. You know what you need and how much you can afford. Behance allows you to contact artists through their platform, but I usually go to email when possible.

About costs: On your first couple projects, your budget may be very tight. Fine. Don't apologize. You're offering work, and the artist makes a professional decision based on their own needs and desires. For low budgets, you may be turned down a couple times before you find the right illustrator. Don't give up on your budget! There are plenty of illustrators who will take your project as a way to build their career.

Your first contact with an illustrator should be a general inquiry asking if they have interest in working on a children's book of a certain kind—include a brief one-paragraph description. If they answer yes, you can provide specs and the manuscript. If they are still interested, you'll move into contract negotiations.

Observation: Often, foreign artists have lower cost of living and can afford to accept a lower payment. I've successfully worked with artists in Great Britain, Poland, Spain, Canada, Ukraine, and Columbia. Payments for overseas artists is usually through PayPal/Xoom or Western Union, but bank transfers are also a possibility.

Negotiate Contracts with Illustrators

The contract that you sign with the illustrator is a legal document. Be sure to have a literary lawyer vet all contracts. Basically, though, everything is negotiable. Go into the process knowing what you want and where you can and cannot budge. Often, the only thing an illustrator asks for is a bigger payment, so be ready with a counter offer and know your absolute limit, past which you'll have to look for a different illustrator.

For signing the contract, use SignNow, DocuSign, or a similar online service that manages the document signing process smoothly. A digital signing service also makes it easy to work with someone overseas. In the U.S., these online signatures have been considered a legal signature since 2000.

Working with Your Illustrator

Hurrah! You've signed up an illustrator for *AUGUST FOLLIES*. Now what?

First, deliver any reference material. My books are often nonfiction, which require the illustrator to use reference photos. For example, *The Nantucket Sea Monster* is based on a true event for which there is great documentation.

Because I work with internationals, I usually send large files through WeTransfer.com, DropBox, or a similar service. Look for a service that works worldwide and is a simple process. Also, discuss with the illustrator how they prefer to communicate: email, phone calls, or video calls.

Next, answer questions. There are always questions about the story, the reference material, your preferences, and so on. Be available and prompt in communicating with the artist, and in return, they'll be prompt and available. I've found that good communication is one of the most important things to making a project work well.

Storyboard or thumbnail sketches (optional). Some authors prefer to give the illustrator a thumbnail layout of the book, or a storyboard. This is just a rough layout of the story, as you envision it. Stick figures are fine, because you're just indicating placement and pacing of the story. I prefer to let the illustrator start the process, but you can choose the working method that you prefer.

Sketches Phase

I find the sketches phase to be exciting. The illustrator divides the text into pages, or follows your instructions on text placement. They do loose, black and white sketches that show layout and composition. Each artist works differently and has different sketching styles. I prefer that the art is placed into the interior book template on InDesign (professional software for print layout), so I can visualize the final book. Another good option is to use a thumbnail layout for picture books (Use Google to find a wide variety of thumbnail layouts.)

When you receive the sketches, it's the first time to see the artist's vision of the book. It's an exciting moment. But also, it's a terrifying moment. Inevitably, the artist's vision doesn't match your vision. You must try to put aside your ideas and embrace the artist's ideas. It's a matter of respect for the artist's professional skills and vision. And it's a delicate moment for the book itself. You and the artist are working toward the same goal, a great book. You may ask for changes on anything! But should you?

Here are things I look at in the sketches phase.

Layout. Is the page layout and composition pleasing? Does it support the story? (See Molly Bang's book in the resources below for more on composition.)

Text placement. In the West, we read picture book text left to right and top to bottom. On a double-page spread, say pages 2-3, the text flow is top left, bottom left, top right, bottom right. You can skip any of those or indeed, just use one placement. The sketches should indicate somehow where the text will be placed. Just be sure the story flows across the page correctly.

Gutter. When books are printed and bound, the binding takes some room. The area near the center binding is called the gutter. Nothing important should be placed near the gutter: art elements, text, or important design elements. Artists can get lost in the composition and forget that the double-page spread must accommodate that gutter. Usually book interior templates account for this and push important elements away, but I always check gutters in the sketch phase.

Storytelling. There's a big difference in a great artist and a great illustrator. The illustrator works to add emotions and to fill out the story. Their art conveys character, action, and setting. This is the time to make sure that the story is told in both art and text.

Page Turns. Often when I write a picture book manuscript, I'll work to add an exciting page turn. In other words, the text is divided up in such a way that the reader is compelled to turn the page. Sometimes, you can divide a sentence in half and finish it on the next double-page spread. The first half makes the reader want to find out what happens next, and the page turn reveals the answer. These are often set up with leading words: Until, Then, But. During the sketch phase, I like to reevaluate all page turns and create the most interesting turns possible.

Pacing. When you divide a picture book text, you may end up with lots of text on one double-page spread and only a single sentence or a single word on another spread. This pacing of the story makes the reader speed up, slow down, pay attention, gasp or shiver, or any number of emotional responses. Now's the time to enhance story suspense by pacing the illustrations.

The sketches stage is crucial for creating synergy between the art and the words to create a great picture book. In *The Nantucket Sea Monster* picture book, I realized that we could create a combination of a great page turn and a wordless spread. The wordless spread allows readers to take in the sea monster before the page turn reveals a surprise. The wordless spread was crucial to the pacing of the story.

Climax & emotional moments. Likewise, check the

emotional build-up of the story. Important emotional moments need to be signaled in the art somehow, through composition, colors, character actions, characters' faces and expressions, and so on. The climax needs to cover several pages and build to the biggest actions that leave the biggest impact.

Visual Subplot. Some illustrators love to add a visual subplot. Perhaps a mouse is shown in each spread and its actions constitute a subplot. Check to be sure the subplot is integral to the written story and enhances it in some way. It may need tweaking so the visual subplot has a story climax, good pacing, and so on.

Cover. The cover is your book's most important sales tool. Now is the time to try out different fonts, text placement, etc. That way, the art will fit with the cover layout. Don't wait for these crucial decisions until the art comes in. That's too late. Also, shrink the cover image to a tiny size such as you'd see on an online bookstore. Can you still read the text, and does it create an impact?

Orientation. Everything should **point to the right**, leading the reader through the book. For example, characters, animals and other important elements should be pointed right. Everyone travels from left to right. They say that in advertising, all elements point the art to the product. But in a picture book, the goal is to lead the reader through the story. Sometimes, two characters face off and it's hard to point right, so then use your judgment.

I've been in lectures with art directors, and some tend to be obsessive over this. For example, one art director showed an image of a lake with the main bird facing right. He asked for the artist to revise by turning all the background birds to also face right. When he showed the before and after, it was fascinating to see how the art had a stronger pull toward the page turn.

For nonfiction children's books, everything must be factual. In my book, *Pelorus Jack, the New Zealand Dolphin,* the steamships, the clothing, the surrounding area of New Zealand's French Pass and Pelorus Sound must be as realistic as possible. The illustrator is responsible for finding reference material, but I often provide material I found during research. That makes it easier for the illustrator and helps you document the facts from the illustrations.

Please do not add any text to images. Sometimes, I ask for a diagram or an illustration that will be labeled. For example, the technical illustration of the dolphin in *Pelorus Jack, the New Zealand Dolphin* had to correctly show the anatomy of the Risso's dolphin. I planned to label the diagram with important anatomical features. But I don't want the illustrator to do that. The text must always be on a separate Photoshop layer so it can be edited. If the copyeditor finds an error, I must be able to correct it. Also, the font for the text is part of the book's design and should be consistent with the rest of the design. Finally, if the book is translated, diagram labels must also be translated. For those reasons, I don't allow the illustrator to add text to images, unless they are on a separate, editable layer.

Full bleed. My picture books usually have a full bleed, which means the art goes up to the edge of the book. Typically, a printer wants an extra 0.125″ of extra art going past the book's edge. That is called the book's bleed. When art is turned in, you should check that it is the correct size, and includes the appropriate bleed required by your printer.

What I'm NOT Suggesting

Notice that I'm not suggesting all sorts of changes: color of a scarf, clothing worn by the main character, type of house, and so on. Those decisions belong to the illustrator unless they are crucial to the story and its plot. For example, if the story takes place in a large apartment complex and the illustrator provides a farm setting, then you'll need to talk. Otherwise, it's the illustrator's decision. I'm only looking at the structure and layout particular to a picture book and to storytelling for kids.

I often send a detailed set of comments on the sketches. Professional artists will accept the input and make changes. You may or may not need to see revised sketches. Be respectful of their time, and don't demand a new look for small things that can be easily changed. Only request it when there are major changes that need to be finalized. Sometimes, I only get a new sketch for a couple pages.

If you miss something in the sketches phase, it's not the end of the world. But it certainly is easier to make changes at this stage. After an illustrator spends time on the color art, it's much harder to change.

Once the sketches are approved, be prompt at paying the installment for this stage of the art. Your illustrator will thank you for promptness.

While the Illustrator Finishes Color Art

Usually artists send me a couple updates during the process of creating the final color art. I like it best when they put the art into the InDesign template and create a low-resolution pdf to send. Or, I'm glad to look at an .indd file (InDesign). But you may prefer to just see jpegs or images of each page. Figure out what works best for you!

It's good to touch base now and then because this can take a long time, depending on the artist's style and other projects. Of course, I'm always available to answer questions. Be a cheerleader for the artist and celebrate every milestone.

Problems Working with Illustrators

When you work with a talented illustrator, you need to keep in mind that they are professionals trying to earn a living. When problems arise—and they often arise—work through the problems with respect and professionalism.

You want to change the specs. Let's say that you've been getting bids from printers and decide to change the finished trim size from 8.5″ × 8.5″ to 8.5″ × 11″. That's the sort of thing that might legitimately happen. Unfortunately, you signed a contract based on the first specs. It's not fair to change the specs in any way without extra payment. Any changes should be in writing and a substantial change order would include extra fees. Be very sure of your specs before you sign that contract.

Deadline not met. Late art is another common problem. When I set up a timeline for a book's production, it's not random. It's based on deadlines for submission to distribution partners, review journals, and the marketplace. It means I must change the launch timeline, which may affect other books, my plans for timed releases, and personal plans.

You'll have to decide how to deal with this on a case by case basis. Why is the art late? Illnesses, natural disasters, and so on are excusable, if irritating. But if the artist is simply not working and you've seen no art at all, you may need to consider terminating the contract. It's not fun, but the process should be in your contract. Work with artists when possible, but remember that you're a businessperson and make decisions accordingly.

Personal problems. One of my best illustrators had twin boys. Besides the difficult last days of pregnancy, it meant about two years when her focus was on her family. It happens. Emotional problems, divorce, surgery for a spouse, break up of a relationship—life often interferes with the artistic process. Again, deal with these on a case by case basis. For the mother of twins, I waited two years for art because my project was book four of a series, and I loved her work.

Disappointing final art. What if you've gone through the whole process and you look at the final art and cringe? Should you publish it anyway? This is a personal, professional and business decision that you'll have to figure out for yourself.

If you've paid for the final art, you've kept your end of the contract. But you always have the option to simply not publish and to go back and look for new illustrations. If you haven't approved the final art and are withholding the last payment, try to work with the illustrator. Sometimes, it's not possible and you must make a decision about the payment. Be respectful when possible and remember that they have families to feed, too. But if you've given direction that was ignored, it may be time for a hard decision.

It goes back to what we started with: Does the finished book create the right reader experience for your story? If it does, publish.

If it doesn't, stop. Think. Decide what to do next.

Indie novelists have an easier time choosing art. They only have to deal with cover art, the sales tool. Children's picture books, however, must consider how storytelling meshes text and words into a gestalt experience. If you publish a children's picture book, you need a great vision for the story and the crucial skills of finding and working with great illustrators.

Support the Illustrators!

Finally, I'll say that one of the art director's jobs is to cheer on the illustrator. They work hard, pouring time and passion into a project. I try to lavish them with praise. When reviews come in, I send them excerpts of the notes about the illustrations. I look for promotional efforts that can benefit them.

Peter Willis, the illustrator of the Moments in Science series, has twice been featured by the Children's Book Council's celebration of Children's Book Week. They asked him to create coloring or art pages for kids. As a result, we blogged about his art for a week.

Becoming a great art director is an ongoing goal for me. I visit art museums to study great art, read lots of picture books, and try to create art in many forms. I do all that because I love the visual mediums. But it all feeds into the work I do as an art director.

Resources

The more you understand about the process of illustrating a children's picture book, the better you'll be able to direct the artist. Here are some starting points.

Blogs

• Shelley, John. Picture Book Basics — Understanding Format. Words & Pictures Blog, Online Magazine of the SCBWI British

Isles.   http://www.wordsandpics.org/2013/07/picture-book-basics-understanding-format.html

• Shelley, John. Picture Book Basics — Sketches and Layout. Words & Pictures Blog, Online Magazine of the SCBWI British Isles.   http://www.wordsandpics.org/2013/08/picture-book-basics-sketches-and-layout.html

• The Design of a Picture Book blog has many interesting posts on picture books, including layout and design. http://designofthepicturebook.com/

• Putting the Picture in Picture Books. https://www.darcypattison.com/writing/picture-books/putting-the-picture-in-picture-books/ Making sure your story is optimized for the illustrator to do their work.

Books

Bang, Molly. *Picture This*. Chronicle Books, c. 2016. Originally published in 1991, this is an excellent book that explains how layout and composition within a page can evoke emotions. I've used this with kids and had amazing results.

• • • • • • •

ACTION: Set up an account with Behance.net and start to favorite some authors or images. Envision your book with several different styles of art.

Decide if you will use InDesign or hire someone to do layout and design. If you decide to hire help, start looking for portfolios and asking around for recommendations.

Look through 100 picture books published in the last five years and imagine that you were the art director. Use the checklist from the Sketches Phase above to evaluate the art.

Part Four

The Book - Formats, Printing and Selling

Now, we are in the weeds, the nitty-gritty of how to bring your books to market. Don't turn back! This may be technical, but you can do it and do it well. Give yourself time to learn the needed skills, and they will pay off for years as your business thrives and exceeds your wildest hopes.

Chapter 20
Choosing Formats

One major decision you must make is what format to publish: eBooks, paperback, hardcover, audio, or a combination of formats. Let's talk about the options and how each works when you're an indie publisher.

What Is a Book?

A book is a bunch of words collected into one place. Traditionally, that's been a paper book with hardcover or paperback covers. Called one of the world's most amazing technologies, the book is a simple, portable, effective way to present ideas, stories, or facts.

But the digital revolution means books can also be words and/or images on some type of screen. The eBook revolution has changed the possibilities of sharing your work. It's complicated, as we shall see, but during the 2020 pandemic many turned to eBooks as a practical way to read.

One major way we understand our world is through our sense of hearing. Harking back to the days of the oral storyteller, audiobook sales are on the rise. The opportunities to sell children's audiobooks is limited, but important.

History of Hardcover. Printed books that have a hard cardboard cover are logically called hardcover books. Traditionally, paper books were printed by offset printing. For this, the images and text—the content of the book—is transferred (offset) to metal plates, and then to a rubber blanket on rollers that are inked. The paper runs under the rollers to be printed. Offset printing is the gold standard for printing quality; every other printing method is judged against it.

Offset printing involves many pre-print steps, and it's only economical for large print runs. Depending on the printer, you must print 500–20,000+ copies to get a good price. This affects your business plan because you must include shipping, warehousing, and fulfillment (sending books to whomever ordered) in your budget.

I recently watched "Miss Potter," the movie based on the life of children's book author and illustrator Beatrix Potter. It's a fascinating look at the life of one of the all-time best selling authors of children's books. When my children were small, I read *The Tale of Peter Rabbit* to them so many times that I've memorized it. "Once upon a time there were four little Rabbits, and their names were - Flopsy, Mopsy, Cottontail, and Peter..."

One line in the movie caught my interest, though. When the publishing company was first discussing her book, Beatrix had definite opinions on how it should be published: black and white illustrations so that the price could be kept low. However, the publisher had another idea on how to keep the price low. The book's color interior pages could all be printed on a single sheet of paper, keeping the price attractively low.

That decision—to design the book for an economical printing model—was genius and partly responsible for Potter's huge popularity. That model is so popular that today, children's picture books which are offset-printed are still designed for printing the whole book on one sheet of paper. That means 32 pages.

Standard offset printing places a children's 32-page picture book on the front and back of a single sheet of paper. 32-page books are the standard in the industry, not because it's the best length for a story, but because the printing is economical. If you publish a 24-page book, you waste paper; if you publish a 37-page paper, the cost is doubled because you must use two pieces of paper per book.

However, because that 32-page length became a standard, there's now, more or less, a standard type story told in children's picture books. In a previous chapter, Who Is Your Audience, we briefly discussed how this affects the writing of your story. For more on writing a children's book, see my book, *How to Write a Children's Picture Book*.

Formatting Options

Before we look at the options, there's one crucial thing to remember. You are the publisher. The companies you work with are just your printers. You are in control of the book publishing program, which means you decide when and where it's printed. Unless you sign an exclusive agreement—don't do that!—you can print with several places at a time and change whenever you like for any reason. You are the publisher; the options below merely describe your choices for getting the book into a specific format.

Offset Printing. An offset printer will use your pdf print-ready files (see the Print Ready Files chapter) to print books. The offset printing method is the gold-standard of quality. You can choose U.S. companies or international companies for high quality. For offset printing, you typically print a large quantity and warehouse. When there's an order, you must pick-and-pack and ship. This business plan is print first, sell later.

Digital Printing. Starting in about 1990, printing technology developed a new way of printing: print-on-demand printing. For digital printing, just look at your home computer. Ink-jet printers print line by line, spraying tiny droplets of ink that when viewed from a distance blend into an image. High quality ink-jet or other digital printers can now print books. They are fast and can do one copy at a time. The quality doesn't quite match that of offset printing, but it's very good and each generation of printers improves quality.

For print-on-demand (POD) printers such as IngramSpark, Lulu, or KDP, your book exists as a digital file until someone places an order. Then—and only then—the book is printed and shipped. This drastically affects your business plan. You set up the digital file with a printer and the printer prints, fulfills, and sends you profits. This business plan is sell first, print later.

With POD printing, any length book is possible. POD printers will typically print an even number of pages from 24+ pages and up. (See each printer for specs.) You aren't tied to the 32-page format. Write and design for any length your story demands.

A caution, though, is that if you ever offset print, 32 pages is still more economical; if you ever anticipate an offset print run, stick with the industry standard 32-page picture book. I've done special printings for Junior Library Guild, subscription box services, and educators' groups. For those print runs, the 32-page format made a huge difference in profits.

The downside of POD is the cost. Because a book is a one-off printing, the printing fees are much higher. The budget works, though, because you don't have to deal with shipping, warehousing, and fulfilling. We'll talk more about pricing books later, because it can be tricky to be profitable with POD. Common paperback POD printers include KDP (Amazon), IngramSpark, and Lulu. Hardcover print-on-demand is available from IngramSpark or Lulu. KDP (Amazon) doesn't offer hardcover POD books in specs that allow for picture books, but longer middle grade or YA novels will work. (Check the specs for each printer.)

eBooks. On November 19, 2007, Amazon launched the Kindle reader and changed literature forever. There were eBook readers before, but Amazon's reach expanded the market to the incredibly diverse and thriving market it is today.

eBooks are simply html files (website files) zipped into a certain format. The container for the files is an ePub file, with standards set by international organizations. (https://idpf.org/epub/30/) There are two kinds of eBooks, either flowable text or fixed format. Novels, even middle grade novels, are usually flowable text, which means that it doesn't matter where the text is shown as long as it's in order. You can increase or decrease font size so that the text reconfigures, or reflows, from page to page. Great for those with vision problems, flowable text is one of the main features of an eBook.

But children's picture books need a fixed format eBook. A typical book has double-page spreads with text on top of illustrations. If you tried to reflow it, one page might show an image and the next page would show text.

Keeping the text and illustrations together requires a different format. Because an eBook is simply html text, some eBooks use CSS (cascading style sheets, a standard way of formatting webpages) to position the illustrations and text boxes. But there's a big problem with this method. There are now dozens of popular eBook devices; some estimate over 100 devices, including the legacy models. Each device shows fixed format eBooks in a particular way, and while there are ePub standards, devices don't uniformly show an eBook the same way. Especially not a fixed format eBook.

To avoid the problem of device compatibility, many children's eBooks use a series of images, with each image a reproduction of a page in a picture book. These can be single pages or double-page spreads. One problem with this solution is that the text can appear too small when read on some devices. If a device allows the reader to pinch-zoom, they can easily enlarge the image when needed. Today, most devices allow for the pinch-zoom, but you still need to consider font size on books destined for eBook formatting.

One of the ongoing problems with eBooks is also the delivery costs. Of all the eBook distributors, only Amazon/Kindle charges download fees of $0.15/MB (This varies from market to market; for all the ins and outs, see here: https://kdp.amazon.com/en_US/help/topic/G200634500). A novel, with no illustrations, will seldom be more than 1MB in size so the download fees are negligible. But a full-color children's eBook can easily be 20MB file size. We'll discuss this more later, but for now, understand that if a file is over 8MB, it's hard to be profitable.

Current eBook distributors include KDP, iBooks, Kobo, Apple, GooglePlay, Overdrive, and many more which can be accessed through aggregators such as Draft2Digital and PublishDrive. We'll discuss these in more detail later.

Audiobooks. A final format is audiobooks, digital audio narrations of the text. For children's picture books, this isn't a strong market because they are so short, which makes it difficult to profitably price an audiobook. Also, picture books depend on the illustrations for fully experiencing and often understanding the story. Audio leaves out the illustrations.

Children's novels are great for audio since they don't need the illustrations. While the audiobook market is growing, it's still weak. Looking at audiobooks overall, the market is bullish on audiobooks for adult fiction and nonfiction. For children's books, the market is influenced strongly by schools who haven't embraced this format fully.

One use of audiobooks is to create Read-to-Me eBook versions. For this specific format, as the story is read, each word is visually highlighted in the eBook. Expensive and time-consuming to produce, these are popular on some platforms. But their overall adoption is slow.

Most indie publishers use either Spotify or ACX to distribute audiobooks. Children's audiobook is also popular on reading apps, either as a Read-to-Me format or simply as audio. And there's a growing number of audio-only devices for kids such as Yoto or Tonies. They each have specific requirements for selling audiobooks on their site, and you'll have to investigate the process at each such company.

What Combination of Formats?

You don't have to publish just one format, though you may choose that option. Traditionally, publishers released a hardcover exclusively for a year. If the book sold well in that format, they might issue a paperback format. Why? Partly, the offset hardcover book was more profitable than paperbacks. But there was also a certain prestige in a hardcover book. If a title went to paperback, it was a sign that it was successful. Less successful books never made it to paperback. Scheduling the release of an eBook version is still variable today. Some prefer to release the eBook first, but some hold it back for a year.

Today you're free to schedule the release of your book in any format in any way you like. Personally, I prefer to release all formats simultaneously. I make about the same profit margin on all formats, so there's no financial advantage to one or the other. I find that those who want hardcover (libraries, schools) are a different audience from those who prefer paperback (parents, classroom teachers). The different formats don't cannibalize each other; instead, my income is amplified by the variety of formats.

You are free to decide which formats to release and in what order! The main question is what does your audience want?

Eight Publishers Types

When thinking about the issue of book formats, here are eight typical ways that indie publishers structure their business. Which one appeals to you? Why? Are you a ninth type of publisher, some hybrid of these? How do you see your publishing company and its books?

Handsome Hardcover. This author (often author-illustrator) only publishes hardcover picture books and sells through Amazon's Fulfill by Amazon (FBA) or one of Amazon's other programs (for more, see: https://sell.amazon.com/sell). Their audience is parents and teachers who buy through Amazon. They spend money on high-quality illustrations, and a large quantity of offset printed books, usually printed overseas. Kickstarter is a favorite funding method because the hardcover inventory is a big upfront investment. School visits often add an income stream.

eBook Teen: This author only publishes eBooks and writes teen urban fantasy or other popular YA genres. She concentrates on reaching teens, so has accounts on popular social media platforms: TikTok (BookTok), Instagram (#bookstagrammer), Facebook, or whatever is currently popular. She spends her money on great covers and online advertising. KU (Kindle Unlimited), Amazon's subscription service, even though it requires exclusive listing, is a strong environment for this author's titles, and she's got a killer mailing list.

Courageous Middle Grade. One of the hardest audiences to reach is the middle grade reader. Unlike teens, you can't reach them on social media. Instead, you must target parents, and fiction is a hard sell. Humor and contemporary novels tend to do better, but success is a book-by-book case. This author offers both eBooks and paperbacks, with paperbacks traditionally selling better. Amazon ads and the Amazon ecosystem are her best friends. Often, though, this author also focuses on school visits as a way to sell books and build an audience.

eBook Kids. This author only creates eBooks of children's picture books. Often the art is minimal, inexpensive, or stock photos. These books often appeal to parents and educators, so they are often about social skills, self-esteem and educational topics. For example, they may publish a book on baby animals with stock photos, and the only text is the name of each animal. It's educational and has a place in a child's life, but it's not something for a hardcover market. KU is an essential strategy, so this author works their Amazon ads and the whole Amazon ecosystem. If the author adds picture books to the mix, they can snag some school visits, too.

Gutsy Jack-of-all-Formats. This author does everything:

eBook, audiobook, paperback and hardcover. Generally, they are all released at the same time (when convenient) or as they are produced. This publisher concentrates on getting the widest distribution possible and follows up on every sales lead; they are often the first indie in a distribution stream. Gutsy Jacks are stingy with money, but will spend it on ads which have a strong ROI (which he monitors daily!). School visits are often profitable.

Niche Nancy. This author has found the perfect niche for her titles. She loves, for example, horse books and horse lovers, and knows exactly when and where to find them. She attends rodeos, horse shows, or other regional or national events to find that audience. She never has to stray outside her narrow world, because it's a rich, rewarding life writing about her passions. Kickstarter is a favorite funding method since she can easily reach horse lovers who are passionate enough to help fund a great book on their favorite topic.

Bookstore Joe. This author has set up an online bookstore to sell titles, that is, direct selling to the customer. He sells eBooks, hardcover, paperback and related merchandise. He's got a killer email list and often spends money on Pinterest, Facebook, TikTok, or other social media ads to keep his traffic levels high. (This one is rare, but growing.)

Teachers-Pay-Teachers Sally. This author focuses on the educational market and has probably been a classroom teacher. The TeachersPayTeachers.com marketplace is perfect for her teacher-focused work. She writes and produces lesson plans for other teachers. Pinterest is a killer source of traffic and sales.

Each author has a valid business plan for reaching the right readers of their books. Can you see that eBook Kids has different needs than Gutsy? eBook Kids only needs to learn marketing on Amazon, only needs to learn to produce Kindle eBooks, and only worries about reaching the teen or kids audience. Gutsy, on the other hand, has the skills needed to produce Kindle, epub, audiobook, paperbacks and hardcovers. Bookstore Joe also does multiple formats, but adds in related merchandise. The variety of formats increases possible sales for these two, but the market isn't as targeted as eBook Teen's or Niche Nancy's.

There are no right or wrong answers. There are only decisions that help you make a profit and keep you happy creatively—or not.

• • • • • • •

ACTION: Based on your long-term goals and your audience, decide what formats you will offer.

Chapter 21
Overseas or POD Printing

Should you print your full-color picture books overseas or use print-on-demand (POD)?

Let's take a hard look at numbers. Yes, math. As a small business, you must keep track of your cost of goods, and in the end, it's all about balancing profits with risks.

First, some terms.

Offset printing means that the book is printed on a large printing press that produces the highest standard of quality. The books are then bound and shipped to a warehouse until they are sent to the distributor for sales and fulfillment. Some indie authors use their homes, garages, or rented space as the warehouse and self-fulfill with post office runs daily.

Print-on-demand means that your book lives as a digital file on a printer's server until someone orders the book. Then it is printed and drop-shipped directly to the customer. KDP, IngramSpark, and Lulu are the biggest POD printers. NOTE: You are the publisher! They are merely your printers.

The question is which method is the most profitable. To understand that, we need to look at the cost to deliver a finished book to the customer.

Offset Printing - Overseas

Printers in China, India, Indonesia, Korea, and other countries are able to offer the lowest cost for printed full-color picture books. Always. For an 8.5″ × 8.5″ full-color hardcover picture book, if you order 5,000 copies and up, the cost will be less than $1.00 USD. However, the books must then be shipped to the U.S. and stored in a warehouse. Let's say that you want to use Amazon's Advantage program to sell the book on the Amazon platform. This is a program that sets you up to deliver books to Amazon for sale.

First, let's set up some typical specifications (specs):

8.5″ × 8.5″, 32 pages, paperback, full-color interior on 80# coated paper, gloss cover:
RETAIL PRICE: $8.99
Typical overseas print + shipping fees = $0.98/book.
AMAZON FEES (Estimated)
Amazon referral fees - $1.35/sale
Fulfillment by Amazon fees - $2.64/sale
Shipping to Amazon's warehouse - $0.50/book
TOTAL FEES = $4.49
Profit: $8.99 - $0.98 (overseas printing) - $4.49 (Amazon fees & shipping) = $3.52 profit/book

---

Of course, you can raise the cost of the book and calculate profits at different prices. Political events may influence shipping costs, and if tariffs are imposed, that can affect the pricing.

POD Printing

Let's compare the offset costs to the POD costs.

POD Printing
>   8.5″ × 8.5″, 32 pages, paperback full-color interior, 70#
coated paper, gloss cover - Print cost = $4.20/book
>   RETAIL PRICE: $8.99
>   AMAZON KDP 40% Distribution fee: $3.60
>   Profit: $8.99 - $4.20 (Printing) - $3.60 (distribution) =
$1.19/book

In this example, POD printing has about half the gross profit of offset printing. The associated Amazon fees are less, but printing is much higher. The actual figures may vary depending on your print size, cost of overseas printing, which POD printer you choose to use, and world events and politics that may affect pricing and shipping. When you decide to print, you should do your own calculations for both scenarios.

One option (recommended) is to raise the retail price on your POD book as follows:

RETAIL PRICE $9.99 - profit $1.79
> $10.99 - profit $2.39
> $11.99 - profit $2.99

If you raise your prices too far, the sales will drop. The trick is finding the sweet spot where you make more profit per book but don't lose too many sales because of high prices. Of course, a well-written, well-illustrated book will be more likely to keep higher sales for higher prices, as it will have a higher perceived value. I recommend at least a $2 profit, or the sale isn't worth it.

What Is Your Time Worth?

This type of calculation always leaves me with one big question. What is my time worth? With a POD sale, I just have to set up the files once, and sales run smoothly in the background.

With offset printing overseas, you must get bids from offshore printers, accept the shipping to the U.S., and administer the shipment from your warehouse to Amazon's fulfillment center. The administrative time required would be variable and would presumably get easier as you repeat the process and become streamlined.

I prefer to accept a lower profit by using POD so that I can spend more time writing. I believe that the more books I write and publish, my overall profits will rise. If I'm constantly worrying about administration tasks, I have less time to write. It's a choice you can make for yourself.

Advantages and Disadvantages of Each Printing Option

Beyond just a straight comparison of costs, there are other considerations.

1) Initial Investment.

POD requires minimal upfront investment of cash. For those early in their careers, it means a simple entry into the market. What other type of business allows you to enter the market for such minimal upfront investment?

Offset printing requires large—and risky—outlays of money to print because this type of printing is only profitable on large orders. The larger the order, the smaller the per-book costs. If you print 20,000 books upfront, your per-book cost plummets, but your risks increase because you have 20,000 books to market to recoup your investment.

2) Ongoing Costs. POD has no ongoing costs, because your book is just a digital file until it is ordered. Offset printing, however, means you must warehouse and ship to your distribution center or to Amazon. These have associated fees and administration time involved.

3) Quality of printing. Offset printing is the gold standard and will always be of higher quality. However, POD printing has improved dramatically, and the quality is quite high.

4) Special Printing. If you want to do a board book, popup book, or other book with special printing needs, you'll have to do an offset printing. POD printers only do a normal type of book. Today, they have added many more options such as foil on covers, color end sheets, spray-painted edges, ribbons, and so on. But it's still cheaper with offset printing.

Offset and POD?

Can you do both offset printing and POD? Of course.

YOU are the publisher! You are free to take your files wherever you want, whenever you want, for any reason. You answer to no one but yourself (and your budget!).

For beginning indie publishers, I'd recommend starting with POD printing because it has less upfront costs. Also, you don't know which of your books will sell best until you've done a couple. If at some point you have a runaway best seller, you can always switch to offset printing. If you're selling 1,000 copies of a title per month—consistently—you may want to print a year's supply of 12,000 so you can take advantage of the higher profit margins. But until you know your sales figures, it's risky to print large quantities. As we all know, marketing is the hardest part of this business, and the market can be volatile (witness the ups and downs during COVID). Manage the risks that come to new indie publishers with POD until you have proven successes that you can take to offset.

For experienced indie publishers who can project their sales figures with some accuracy, offset printing makes sense. The margins are higher and profit is larger. It does mean more administrative tasks, but perhaps you can hire help at that point. However, keep in mind that printing in volume is risky. Keep enough reserves in your budget to survive a big loss.

At any stage, if you receive a large order, consider offset printing. One year, I had one order of 1,653 books that I fulfilled with a POD order because they needed the books within two weeks. On the other hand, I've had orders for 5,000 books for which I used offset printing, while also keeping the books available through POD to Amazon and other distributors. For the large order, they gave me a three-month deadline for delivery, which allowed me the extra time needed to set up files with a U.S. offset printer who could then ship to my customer on time. The profit was higher because the per-book costs were lower, and it was a direct order (bypassing a distribution platform such as Amazon). For an overseas printer and potentially even higher profits, I'd likely need an even longer lead time.

You are the publisher. You set your budgets, decide on your profit margins, and make any printing changes whenever you need, however you need. You are in control.

· · · · · · ·

ACTION: Decide on your basic business plan. Will you use POD printing (sell first, print later) or offset printing (print first, sell later)? Of course, you can use POD printing most of the time, but use an offset for bulk orders. Here, though, the question is what is your basic business plan, POD or offset?

Chapter 22
Working With POD Printers

H ere's the thing: current print on demand (POD) printers do not equal the quality of an offset printer—yet. It's very close and each year the gap narrows. Still, there are differences and we need to make allowances for the POD process.

Designing for POD Quality

When you design a book for POD printers, paper quality can vary greatly. Most printers offer a #50, #70, or #80 paper. The # here means pounds. A ream of paper, or 500 sheets, before it is cut into a certain size, would weigh 50, 70, or 80 pounds. #50 or #70 papers are rough, which is fine for black and white novels. However, color printing requires heavier paper.

Ingram and KDP use #70 paper for standard color printing. If you move up to premium printing, the paper quality is heavier. The best POD printing for full-color picture books comes from a coated paper that has (wait for it) a coating that creates a smooth surface. Lulu.com offers an 80# coated paper, which produces better results, but their pricing is higher. Lulu pricing works best when it's the back end of a Shopify store (or Woocommerce or other platform that offers storefronts) because then Lulu doesn't charge distribution costs since your Shopify store is the distribution channel. And KDP's premium printing is on a slightly heavier paper.

In other words, all things being equal, we'd all choose to print on premium papers. But the cost is too high, especially for paperback books. Sometimes, I'll choose Standard70 at Ingram to keep profits high.

If you choose a slightly lighter weight paper, here are some things to do to improve print results.

6 Ways to Optimize Illustrations for POD Printing

1. **Try spot illustrations.** Do you need to fill up the entire page with the art? Ask the illustrator for illustrations that use less ink. This will mean white (unprinted) backgrounds whenever possible. Spot art, small self-contained vignettes, will print the best for POD. Use lots of open space.
2. **Avoid dark or black backgrounds.** For POD printing, black is often diluted to just a dark gray. Also, if you fill the page with ink, lighter papers tend to wrinkle when they dry. If you really must choose dark or black backgrounds, choose the highest quality paper possible. The 80# coated paper from Lulu is a delight after the uncoated paper of other POD printers.
3. **Avoid design elements that must be positioned exactly.** While POD is a great technology, sometimes, the paper isn't aligned perfectly in the printer. That means elements don't line up exactly with the edge of the paper. The most common mistake is a line of white paper at the bottom of the page. Be sure you add the required bleed (usually an added 0.125" all

around the book to allow for imprecise printing), and be sure you click to include the bleed when you export the PDF file. Sometimes, the hardcover book cover is shifted slightly, so the words on the spine aren't centered. To address this, if you number the books in a series, don't put that small number on the book's spine and expect it to look perfect every time. Instead, put that on the book's front or back cover, where exact positioning isn't as crucial. Use a smaller font that will still look good if slightly offset.

4. **Accept the quality of POD printing.** I've never had a teacher or parent comment on the quality of the printing. People do know quality of printing. But when they order books from a school book fair, they understand that the cheaper price means cheaper paper. They understand that printing varies and price can vary depending on the quality of the printing. They do comment on the story, the content of the book. But unless there's a gross misprint, they won't care. I find misprints to be rare; and the printer will always replace them free.

5. **Offset print.** You can abandon the POD business model for certain books or certain orders. That creates multiple problems of warehousing, fulfillment of orders, and so on. Think carefully before abandoning a business model for a single title. For large special orders going to one company, it might be a feasible option.

6. **Don't publish your book.** Maybe it's a good idea to wait until you can switch to an offset business model to publish this particular title. Or, there's nothing that says you must self-publish every book. Perhaps this is the one title for which you seek a traditional publisher.

POD is a viable business plan for indie publishers of children's books. But you should keep in mind the limitations of the POD printing process. You can work within the challenges of the POD printing process to create great books!

• • • • • • •

ACTION: Find some books printed with a POD printer. Look at the quality and decide if the image quality will suit your needs. As you design your next book, plan to accommodate the needs of a POD printer.

Chapter 23
Print Ready Files

A question I often see is some variation of this: I have illustrations from the artist, now how do I get the book printed?

So, let's back up and go through the process of getting print-ready files.

Trim Size

First, before you hire an illustrator, you need to decide on a trim size, the finished size of the book. This decision means you must know ahead where you plan to print the book, or else you must know standard trim sizes. Any nonstandard size will cost much more to print and will cut into your profit. It's always better to stick with a standard trim size.

There are three main POD printers: KDP, IngramSpark, and Lulu. You'll see lists with other companies, and I've tried them all. I stick with these POD printers because they fit my needs the best.

KDP is Amazon.com's POD printing arm, and books set up with KDP will automatically be included in Amazon.com's catalog. If you choose Extended Distribution, KDP sends your book to Ingram for further distribution; generally, I don't recommend Extended Distribution since it adds an extra fee and reduces the profitability of your book.

IngramSpark is the sister company of Ingram Wholesale, the U.S.'s largest book wholesaler. If you POD with IngramSpark, your books are automatically included in Amazon.com's catalog, Ingram Wholesale's catalog, and generally available for any book retailer. In addition, IngramSpark gives you access to a worldwide market of booksellers. Some self-publishers only list books with IngramSpark because its distribution includes Amazon.com, as well as most other distributors. However, IngramSpark and KDP don't always work well together; I find it best to set up books at both POD companies to ensure the best availability.

Lulu.com is an amazing POD printer because they offer a lovely #80 coated paper, perfect for children's picture books, and have excellent customer service. When Lulu.com powers the backend of a Shopify store (or Woocommerce store), the books available are beautiful. I don't recommend Lulu for general distribution because the added fees make the books too expensive. But when you decide to go for direct sales on a Shopify store, Lulu.com is gold.

Each POD company offers a specific list of trim sizes. You must know which POD printer you plan to use so you can choose the right trim sizes. Sadly, I've heard from self-publishers who receive final art only to find out that the art's trim size is not available from the POD companies they plan to work with. They must either ask for revised art and pay for the revisions, or they must turn to offset printers who can print any size, often at increased costs.

KDP, IngramSpark, and Lulu trim sizes

Though it varies widely, for novels, most self-publishers use 5″ × 8″, 5.5″ × 8.5″, or 6″ × 9″. Popular sizes for picture books include 8.5″ × 8.5″, 8″ × 8″, and 8.5″ × 11″.

Let's assume for this discussion that you are publishing a children's picture book and decide to use the 8.5″ × 8.5″ trim size.

Now, you're ready to give your illustrator a spec sheet (list of specifications) for the project. Here's an example that can be varied to meet your needs and your printer's specifications (which can vary).

Project: Great Picture Book

Specifications for the Illustrator

32 pages, 8.5″ × 8.5″ with 0.125″ bleed all around (check printer's specs for exact bleed requirements; often you can download templates for covers).

14 double-spread illustrations, plus one single image for page 32, and background for copyright or dedication page.

Double-spread cover, with the exterior cover doubling for page 1 or interior cover.

All images must be 300 dpi, print ready, provided as jpegs, tiffs, and/or psd.

Add any details about payment schedule, due dates, etc.

Bleed - Printing can vary by hundredths of an inch, and to prevent tiny white lines around the edges of a book, the printer requires that images extend beyond the borders of the book for about 0.125″. This gives them some small allowance for variations. Check your printer's specs for the exact amount of bleed required.

300 dpi - One measure of the quality of an image is dpi or dots per inch. For print, the standard is 300 dpi. For ebooks, the standard is 72 dpi. All photo formatting programs can downsize, or change the 300 dpi to 72 dpi, without a loss of quality, but you can't go the opposite direction. If your images start at 72 dpi, you can't change to 300 dpi, or the image will pixelate, and the quality is low. Therefore, require all art at the highest dpi needed and convert as needed for the ebooks. (If you don't follow this discussion, you'll have to read elsewhere about image quality, as it's beyond the scope of this book.)

Layout and Design

With correctly sized illustrations in hand, you can turn to layout and design. Of course, you'll be thinking about this as the illustrations are developed. I'll cover it here as a separate step, but it's really integral to the illustrations step.

Layout refers to how the images are integrated with the text, and it's an art form. The illustrator should have allowed space for the text, or you may have planned to add colored boxes for text. All of the planning for the trim size, art direction, and integration with the text is referred to as the book's design. This is a vast topic, the subject of many books and courses. For a simple introduction to it, I recommend *The Non-Designer's Design Book* by Robin Williams. But know that you'll always be learning how to improve your layout and design.

For a novel, you'll worry about page numbers, page headers, and margins. For newbies, I highly recommend that you buy and use a template, such as those from BookDesignTemplates.com. They set up everything for you in either Word or InDesign. For a quick reference on industry standards for book layout, refer to the IBPA's Industry Standards Checklist. (https://www.ibpa-online.org/general/custom.asp?page=standardschecklist)

As an alternative, use the Vellum program (for Mac only) or the Atticus program (for PC, Mac, or Linux) to layout both ebook and print at the same time. The templates are limited, but professional. If you're doing both digital and print, this may be the best solution.

For picture books, however, I highly recommend Adobe's InDesign program because it's the industry standard for creating professionally designed books. At the time of writing, it's a $21.99 monthly subscription based on a single-app subscription rate; they prefer you purchase a multi-app subscription, so you may have to look for the single-app option. BTW, one seldom-known advantage of the InDesign subscription is that you also have access to Adobe fonts and can use them for any project.

The learning curve for InDesign is steep, but I recommend you persevere in learning the program so you're not always at the mercy of others. Also, as I've done foreign rights, the foreign publishers expect to receive InDesign files.

The alternatives to InDesign are poor: Microsoft Word, Canva, PowerPoint, etc. In my opinion, they lack the design capabilities to produce the best layouts at the best quality. The one alternative that I'd recommend is Affinity Publisher, an InDesign lookalike from a British company. It's a one-time purchase of about $50 (at the time of writing), and the program's development is robust and ongoing. Notice that you won't have access to Adobe's fonts. You'll have to pay for fonts you choose to use.

The design process can take anywhere from one day to a month, depending on the book's complexity, your skill and experience, and your level of perfectionism. Take the time to get this right, so the book will have the best possibility of success. I should probably repeat that 100 times!

Fonts are often debated hotly among self-publishers. There is no required font, just what looks pleasing with the illustrations and fits the tone of the book. For children's picture books, I recommend at least 14 pt, but it can go much larger, depending on the story's length and the layout. Fonts for novels usually range from 11 pt to 14 pt. (For more, see: https://www.indiekidsbooks.com/p/what-fonts-for-childrens-books)

Exporting the PDF

Printers require a print-ready PDF. InDesign exports easily in any PDF format required. Usually, the PDF/X-1a:2001 standard is sufficient for print-ready files. Some printers will also accept the PDF/X-3:2002 standard or a later standard. These standards are presets that ensure the files are high quality; if you use a nonstandard program, you still need to make sure the files match that quality standard.

MS Word will export the standard PDFs only if your system includes an Adobe add-in that facilitates the exports. Unfortunately, that add-in isn't commercially available. It's often included, though, in tax or accounting software, so your system may have it. To check, open a Word document, then click PRINT. At the bottom left, click on the PDF option. You'll want the "Save as Adobe PDF" option to get the correct options for print-ready files.

InDesign has a Preflight Panel that checks all the files for compatibility with the printing process. Be sure to run this before exporting.

I label the print-ready PDF files with the ISBN number and a one-word truncated title for easy identification.

You'll need a separate file for the interior and for the cover. Be sure to look through the entire file before uploading to a printer. This is your last chance to catch mistakes.

Resources

Need more specific help? I recommend this book:

Raven, Fiona, and Glenna Collett. *Book Design Made Simple.* They also have a blog at BookDesignMadeSimple.com

• • • • • • •

ACTION: When you have final art, create or ask your designer to create print-ready files.

Chapter 24
Distributing Children's eBooks

Reading apps rule!

Children's book authors concentrate on print books for good reasons. For most people, 80–90 percent of sales for children's books are paperback, with a few hardcovers and a few ebooks or audiobooks thrown in.

So, what do we do with those digital files, ebooks and audiobooks?

I've had success in going to reading apps for kids. In this chapter, I'll explain where and how you can distribute your ebooks and audiobooks.

Why Reading Apps?

First, let's talk about why reading apps are so important: customer behavior. Everyone who reads ebooks or listens to audiobooks has their favorite apps. Because the files are digital, readers or listeners need a place to store the files that also gives them handy access. For children's books, this is especially important because kids need a simple interface. Yes, they are GenAlpha and are first-generation digital natives, but they are young and still need a relatively simple interface to consistently access their data.

There's also the cost. Would you rather buy a kid one ebook at $5.99, or purchase a subscription for $9.99 that allows them access to unlimited reading of over 40,000 books? It's a no-brainer.

When people say that kids don't read ebooks, I laugh. Remember when we discussed the EPIC! reading app that had a billion reads in 2020? Kids read ebooks; they just do it on apps. It's easy, cost-effective, and gives kids a huge selection of books. It's a digital library in a single app. When apps gamify the experience with badges, avatars, and interactive reading comprehension questions, it's even more likely that kids will spend time on the app.

One advantage of a reading app is the variety and range of choices. Kids are usually self-selecting books to read. I'd love to see studies that look at this—but most of the research on ebooks is focused on whether kids should read digitally. That ship has sailed. A billion reads.

As independent publishers, then, how can we reach this vast audience? Here's one distributor and two apps that can help boost your sales.

eBook Files

PDF or ePub. For ebooks, good news. We struggle to create ebooks from our full-color picture books. But the apps often just want a high-resolution PDF that they can adapt to their proprietary platform. If you find a platform that does need an ePub, see the chapter on ePub - Creating Files. Usually, an app will ask for metadata delivered in their proprietary spreadsheet format. You'll just need to cut and paste the metadata information from your standard spreadsheet.

Distribution

KDP—Amazon ebooks and Kindle Unlimited. Kindle Unlimited is Amazon's "reading app" or unlimited reading program that kids can take advantage of. If you place your books into KU, you have the possibility of reaching thousands of kids. KU provides a couple marketing tools such as Kindle Countdown. If you choose this route, you'll want to use the appropriate format to create your ebooks. There are many posts on how adult fiction or nonfiction works in KU, so read those and adapt to your books.

The big disadvantage is that KU requires that you keep your ebooks exclusive to them. I've never done KU because I've always had my books in Overdrive or the EPIC! reading app, so I can't go exclusive to KU. But if you choose to go with KU, it can be lucrative for the right books. Join KU and try it out. It's easy to opt in and opt out at will.

BTW, this is the origin of the phrase "going wide." When KU started, it was the only option for reaching readers quickly. But as other options grew, you "went wide" when you took your ebooks out of the exclusive KU and enrolled them on other platforms.

To enroll in Kindle Unlimited, visit your KDP Dashboard for full information. (For more, see the chapter KU or Wide.)

D2D—aggregator of ebooks. An aggregator takes your ebook and/or audiobook and distributes to a wide range of platforms, both national and international. Draft2Digital (D2D) puts ebooks on U.S. and international platforms and delivers profits.

Overdrive—direct to distributor. Overdrive is a world-wide provider of audiobooks and ebooks, mostly to libraries. They use the Libby app for public libraries and the Sora app for schools. It's a thrill to see sales in South Africa, Indonesia, or Ireland.

Most people send files to Overdrive through Draft2Digital or Kobo, but I've always gone direct. And I've been direct with them for years. The first time I applied, I was turned down, but a couple months later I was asked to apply. I think someone had requested my books through the platform.

For many years, the books limped along with about $1,000 in sales/year. In 2023, though, Overdrive assigned me a rep, and the income was 5× higher. About 35 percent is audiobook sales and 65 percent ebook sales. When the rep manages to place an ad for your book in the coveted monthly mailing, sales soar.

SUGGESTION: Spend a month asking people to request your books through their library for the Libby app, which is Overdrive's app used in public libraries. Then apply to go direct. I don't know how much it will help, but it's about the only thing that might. Libraries do listen to their patrons.

Overdrive requires ePub files, audiobook files, and cover files, along with their proprietary spreadsheet for metadata. Instructions are easy to read. Publishers are paid quarterly.

Apply to Overdrive here: company.overdrive.com/publishers/

EPIC! The biggest reading app in the U.S. is EPIC! After about ten years in business, it's in 90 percent of school libraries, and teachers and school librarians love it for its ease of use, wide and diverse catalog, and pricing—it's free for school librarians and teachers to use. It's a brilliant marketing strategy where the program is free to educators, but then the educators assign kids to read something on EPIC! And parents subscribe. The teacher recommendation has driven huge adoption across the U.S.

However, the EPIC! company was bought out by an Indian company in 2020, and that company filed for bankruptcy in 2024 to bring the business back to the U.S. In 2025, EPIC! will be sold and no one knows what that will mean. It's business as usual for now, but stay tuned.

EPIC! accounts for about one-third of my income overall. One book series, *A Little Bit of Dinosaur* series, is a breakout on the platform with over 6 million reads! Payment is pennies per read, but at 6 million reads, it adds up.

It's an app to watch, but it's not one that is easily reached. They require a backlist of 50 titles. When I was accepted years ago, you only needed 20–25 titles. If you have close to 50 titles, check it out.

Booka. A new exciting reading app appeared on the iPhone App Store in 2022. Booka is an app recommended for preschool and early elementary readers. EPIC! has the school library market wrapped up, so Booka reaches out to parents and grandparents directly.

Let me emphasize that you should look at the type of books on each app. Booka's titles are simpler books for lower elementary levels. My nonfiction science books struggle to do well here, but titles like *Goldilocks: The Name-Fame Dame* and *A Little Bit of Dinosaur* are doing well.

I highly recommend you download prospective apps and sign up for a month to see the type of books they offer. (I keep saying this—it's important!)

AppBooka is easy to work with, requiring a simple upload of PDF/audio files/cover file and a metadata spreadsheet. Payment is quarterly and the income is small but reasonable. And growing. They are new and tell me that they are growing subscribers by 10 percent/month. That sounds great. The company is based in Cyprus, but the app is generally available in the U.S. app stores and a growing number of other countries.

Other eBook Platforms. Stay tuned. Every year, I see a new ebook platform for kids pop up. I try them all! When a technology company has a great idea to create an ebook platform for kids, they may execute the tech part great, but they need content. For that, they must come to us. Keep an eye out for new options.

Recommendations for eBook Distribution

When you submit to apps, concentrate on a catalog of books because they don't want to set up everything for just one book. There's no hard and fast rule for the depth of your backlist, but think about what they need—and try out their app—before you send.

Keep an eye out for startup reading and/or audiobook apps. The time to get in is early in their life cycle. Some will never succeed, but some will. It's a low risk for us to put our books on their platforms, as long as it's not exclusive and the terms are reasonable. Periodically check my blog at IndieKidsBooks.com for updates on distributors.

• • • • • • •

ACTION: List the companies you plan to use for book distribution. Create accounts with these companies so the uploading process will be simple.

Chapter 25
Creating ePubs

An ePub is the standard format for ebooks. But children's picture books as ePubs are difficult. Why? Most ebooks are reflowable ebooks. That is, if you increase or decrease the text size (as allowed by most ebook readers), the text reflows smoothly to the next page. This is appropriate for most novels, including young adult novels, middle grade novels, and short chapter novels. For these ebooks, I recommend Vellum (Mac) or Atticus (PC, Mac, or Linux) to format.

Picture books, however, don't have reflowable text. Instead, the text is embedded into the image, and indeed a particular text must be next to a certain image for the story to be understood properly. They really aren't made for the ebook format. However, we've found ways to make it work by creating fixed format ebooks.

The first attempt to create fixed format ebooks requires a slight explanation of an ebook. It's actually just a webpage—html coding—that is zipped into an .epub extension. There are required files that work together to pull the book together to show the book on any given reader. That means the first attempts to create fixed format used CSS, cascading style sheets, which are used for formatting webpages.

It should work. And it does work—on some ebook readers. The problem is that there are over 100+ ebook readers, each programmed to show ebooks in slightly different ways. When I tried this technique, there was no consistency across different ereaders. One would work well, the next would be wonky. It's not reliable.

The second attempt to create fixed format ebooks is to export images, with text embedded, and create ebooks with those images. This method works best, and I'll detail it later.

One other issue comes up when creating fixed format ebooks: file size. When you transform the full-color, high-resolution book to an ebook, the file sizes will be huge unless you manage it well. This means that the book will take up too much room on people's devices and can take a lot of bandwidth to download. And in the next chapter, we'll discuss why it's crucial to reduce ebook sizes for Kindle because they charge download fees.

Creating an ePub Fixed Format eBook

So, what's the recommended workflow to create a fixed format ePub with low file size?

Lower the File Size

First, let's address how to lower the file size, regardless of the program you use. Programs will suggest that you upload your print pdf to the program and it will spit out an ePub. Yes, that happens, but the file sizes are huge. That's a terrible option.

Instead, I choose to export images. I use Adobe's InDesign program for my picture books. Instead of exporting to pdf, I export to jpeg, with each page (or double-page spread) a separate file. Then, I use Photoshop Elements (or any other photo formatting program) and convert the photos to smaller sizes with lower resolutions.

Here are the export specs that I use:

1000 px wide for pages (auto formatting for height). This fits the size of the Kindle screens very well.

72 dpi. For print, you need high resolution of 300 dpi. But for screens, 72 dpi produces a great image.

60% to 70% Quality rating/Medium quality rating. This further reduces the file's size, without sacrificing quality when shown on an eBook screen. Some will argue this setting, but my ebooks always look great on an ebook reader.

I tried exporting single pages, and you can do that. But I choose to reduce file sizes even more by exporting spreads; this means when I create the ebook, I choose to show one page at a time, the double-page spread. When I export the spreads, I choose the 2000px wide (auto height). This means each page is only 1000px wide, while the spread is 2000 px.

The next step is to strip out any extra file size caused by meta-data. I use ImageOptim, a Mac program, but you can find similar PC programs. Look for a program that reduces file size by removing metadata.

You simply drag and drop images to ImageOptim, and it reduces 15%-30% file size by removing metadata.

Now, the optimized images are ready to use in whatever program you prefer.

The Surprising Program that Works - Mac's Pages program

I've experimented with many, many programs to create fixed format ePubs! This one surprised me: Apple's Pages program. Let's look at how it works. If you use a PC, then skip to the next chapter.

Open Pages, and File > Create New > Blank Book.

File > Page Setup. I usually create 8.5″ × 8.5″ square books. So I'll set up a file with 8.5″ pages.

On the right-hand side, click on DOCUMENT > Facing Pages.

This will simulate a double page spread, so you can read the book correctly. Use zero-inch margins all around.

Click on Media > Choose and select the file for the first page of your book. Insert. It will fill up the page almost to the edge. I choose to pull it all the way to the edges because I don't want white edges around the eBook. By default, the program will add a black background around the ePub, and I would find the white border distracting.

Continue to add pages until you've added all the pages in your book!

Create the ePub

Once everything looks great in your file, then it's simple to export.

Export > ePub > Fixed Format. You can choose to use the first page as the cover, or add a cover image. I choose the Category of Children & Teens. View as Two Pages. There's no reason to Embed Fonts or use a Table of Contents, since everything is an image.

Click NEXT and choose (or create) an empty folder for the ePub. Click Export.

Voila! You are done! My ePub file size turned out at 4.5 MB, a good size. Test the file by opening it in Apple's iBooks program.

For a final validation test, I use Draft2Digital's free ePub validator (https://draft2digital.com/book/epubcheck/upload). No errors.

I have tested this ePub on Androids using the GooglePlay app and on Apple devices with iBooks, and it works great on both. In short, we have a simple, easy program to create a fixed format ePub for picture books that works well on iBooks and GooglePlay. I usually recommend that my customers use one of these two programs.

If you don't use a Mac computer, then the next chapter explains how to use the free Kindle Create program to create ePubs.

•••••••

ACTION: If you use a Mac computer, download ImageOptim to reduce file sizes. If you use a PC look for a similar program to remove metadata and reduce file sizes.

Mac users, try creating an epub with MacPages, and then validate the epub.

Chapter 26
Creating EPUBs for Kindle

K indle, an ebook for the Amazon Kindle reader, requires an ePub file, and Amazon makes the ePub creation simple with their Kindle Create app, a free downloadable software. This works well on PC (or Mac) computers and the resulting file can be used anywhere.

Kindle Create

The Kindle Create is a free download here: https://www.amazon. com/Kindle-Create/b?node=18292298011

The Kindle Create program has been around for a long time to create ePubs for things like cookbooks and comics. When layout needs to be exact this is their go-to program. They now recommend that you use it to create children's picture books, which also require exact placement.

They recommend that you start with your print-ready PDF, but I've found that the resulting ePub file sizes are huge . Instead, I optimize as in the previous chapter, and then add the images to the program. If you choose to use pages, choose to use two-page spreads.

If you optimize spreads as your images, choose to use one page per spread (because the two images are already embedded in the image together).

On the starting screen, in the left-hand column, choose KIDS.

On the next page, add the title, author, and publisher.

On the next page, you'll choose how the fixed-format ebook is displayed. Choose either single page (you exported spreads) or facing pages (you exported single pages). Then continue and follow directions.

If you have optimized your images, then the resulting file sizes will be reasonable.

Decide on Your Work Flow

Take some time to try a couple of ways of creating ebooks until you find one you like. Then, stick with it. The important thing here is to minimize decision making for each repetition of the task of creating an ePub. In other words, streamline your work flow. When I finish laying out a book in InDesign, I immediately export Spreads and Pages into separate folders and bulk edit them with Photoshop. Immediately, I optimize the images with ImageOptim. Then, when I'm ready to create ePubs, the raw materials are already done.

Creating fixed-format ePubs is easier than ever with Pages or KindleCreate. You should have ePubs of all your picture books, which adds another income stream—always a good thing.

Caution: Beware of file sizes!

When you publish an ebook on KDP, they add a download fee. Here's what KDP says about current download fees: https://kdp.amazon.com/en_US/help/topic/G200634500#70

Delivery Costs are equal to your file's megabytes multiplied by the Delivery Cost. As I write this book, here are the delivery fees:

Amazon.com: US $0.15/MB

    Amazon.ca: CAD $0.15/MB

    Amazon.com.br: R$0.30/MB

    Amazon.co.uk: UK £0.10/MB

    Amazon.de: €0,12/MB

    Amazon.fr: €0,12/MB

    Amazon.es: €0,12/MB

    Amazon.in: INR ₹7/MB

    Amazon.it: €0,12/MB

    Amazon.nl: €0,12/MB

    Amazon.co.jp: ¥1/MB

    Amazon.com.mx: MXN $1/MB

    Amazon.com.au: AUD $0.15/MB

Once you upload your ebook, you can see the official file size on the pricing page.

If you choose the 70% royalty rate, distribution fees apply. If you choose the 35% royalty rate, there are no distribution fees. Here's a handy chart to calculate the fees.

File size	Delivery Cost@$0.15/MB	@2.99 Download fees	@3.99 Download fees	@4.99 Download fees
8MB	$1.20	40%	30%	24%
7MB	$1.05	35%	26%	21%
6MB	$0.90	30%	22.5%	18%
5MB	$0.75	25%	18.8%	15%
4MB	$0.60	20%	15%	12%
3MB	$0.45	15%	11.3%	9%
2MB	$0.30	10%	7.5%	6%
1MB	$0.15	5%	3.75%	3%

If your ebook is over 8MB in size, then you should opt for the 35% royalty rate or you'll lose money.

Kindle Unlimited

Once you upload your ePub to KDP, you can choose to add your book to Kindle Unlimited. This is Amazon's version of a reading app for kids! If you only distribute ebooks to KDP, then you can opt into KU and take advantage of their marketing programs. Remember that if you distribute anywhere else, you cannot use KU.

KU pays per page read, and the exact amount varies month-to-month. They will assign your book a certain number of pages. If you use KU, I recommend you back up and use Pages to create the ePub not Spreads. With Pages, KU will assign your book 32 pages, but with Spreads, it's likely to be 17 pages. In other words, you'll earn half the amount through KU.

Kindle ePubs dominate the adult market, but can add a nice boost to income for children's books. The file sizes and number of pages in the ebook are crucial to making sure you optimize your income. (See more in the KU v Wide chapter.)

• • • • • • •

ACTION: Download Kindle Create, a free download here: https://www.amazon.com/Kindle-Create/b?node=18292298011

Use the ImageOptim or other PC file-reducing program from the previous chapter. Then, create an epub with Kindle Create.

Chapter 27
Audiobooks

Once you establish sales for print and ebooks, you may be interested in audiobook sales. While the audiobook market for adult titles has grown tremendously, it's a slower growth for children's audio. One reason is the pricing structure on platforms such as Audible. They use credits and then assign credit values to audiobooks. For example, a fantasy novel might include 14 hours of audio, while a children's short chapter novel might include 2 hours of audio. Yet, they both cost "1 credit." The longer fantasy novel is perceived as a better value. And when you try for a 15-minute picture book narration, the market disappears. Still, there are bright spots here and there.

For my picture books, I create audiobooks because the reading apps will use the audio to create read-to-me or other similar formats. For a read-to-me format, each word is highlighted on the screen as it is spoken aloud. Kids can track the text as it's read, which some studies suggest will help them learn to read. Or, for kids who struggle to read, it's still a way to gain experience with the written word by adding the audio component. Not all platforms use read-to-me, but if you work with a platform that does, this format sells well for my books. I don't worry about creating the read-to-me format though; the platform uses their proprietary methods to do this.

For longer novels, I seldom do audiobooks because the cost has been prohibitive. Audiobook narrators earn $50–$400 per finished hour, but great narrators will go higher. A finished hour of audio means all the editing has been done and the audio is ready to upload and sell. An hour of narration could be 8,000–10,000 words, depending on the narrator. If you have a 50,000-word novel, then it would be 4–6 hours of finished audio. At $400/hour of finished audio, that's $1,600–2,400. The question is can you earn that much from a children's novel in audiobook format? For most, the answer has been no.

Audiobook Narrator

Creating audiobooks means hiring someone to narrate the book, that is, read and record it and provide appropriate files. This means you'll need to provide them with a contract for their services. Most narrators use Audacity to edit files, which has a plugin for Audible (Amazon's audiobook platform) standards. In the contract, I ask them to comply with the current Audible requirements for audio quality, a standard that is generally accepted across the industry.

If you choose to record your own books, be sure you can also meet those standards. See the full standards here: https://help.acx.com/s/article/what-are-the-acx-audio-submission-requirements

Finding narrators is tricky. There are companies who provide platforms for narrators to connect with authors, but they usually require you to process the contract on their platform. I've found that just asking friends for recommendations is as reliable as any other method.

I particularly like when I can find a perfect narrator. For example, *Abayomi, the Brazilian Puma* is narrated by David deSantos, a native of South America. While not specifically from Brazil, his accent was perfect for this story.

Pelorus Jack, the New Zealand Dolphin is narrated by Melissa Gunn, who is a native New Zealander. The addition of voices specific to a geographical region add to the charm of these audiobooks.

AI Narration

The use of Artificial Intelligence (A.I.) has been a controversy sweeping through the publishing industry throughout the mid-2020s. I won't debate the pros and cons of it here, letting you go where your convictions lie. Instead, I'll explain what's now available in the audiobook format and let you decide on the best path for your publishing company.

In 2025, ElevenLabs changed the face of A.I.-generated audiobooks by making it easy for the average person to create such audiobooks. On ElevenLabs' audiobook platform, you can choose from a variety of voices, or create a custom voice, including a clone of your own voice. Audiobooks can be accessed on the ElevenLabsReader app, or download the files to make them available on other platforms, too. Most platforms plan to clearly label that these are A.I.-generated files so the listener will know what they are getting.

The real advantage will be cost. Accounts at ElevenLabsReader will be much lower than hiring an individual narrator, making audiobooks available to many more authors. There's still the problem of the customer's perceived value for the shorter children's books, so costs may be low, but income may stay low, too.

Other platforms also allow you to create A.I.-narrated audiobooks, such as GooglePlay and AppleBooks. GooglePlay allows you to download the files and use in other places, but AppleBooks' A.I.-generated audio remains only on their platform.

Check your preferred platform to see their current policies on A.I.-narrated audiobooks.

Selling Audiobooks

While there's now a long list of platforms that sell audiobooks, the problem is that few have an audience for children's books. If you decide to go forward with an audiobook, I have a few words of advice. First, I suggest that you keep an eye on many platforms, but concentrate on a few. Read the Terms of Service and Payment Schedules carefully as there are many ins and outs to the payment schedules. If you choose A.I.-generated files, prepare a disclosure statement for customers.

EPIC! App. This ebook app also provides audiobooks, and they add audio to an ebook to create the popular read-to-me format. The read-to-me formats are consistently my most popular titles.

Findaway/Spotify. Spotify for Authors allows access to this huge, international market. Sadly, it's not been popular for my books.

Overdrive. If you go direct to Overdrive with ebooks, then it's an easy choice to add audiobooks here. It's one of the few places where I consistently get audiobook sales, although the numbers are small.

These platforms also provide audiobook sales that you can investigate: ACX - Amazon, Apple Books, AuthorRepublic, Chirp, GooglePlay, Kobo, Librivox, Scribd, Storytel, and others.

YouTube or Podcasts. Authors of adult books have created a demand for audiobooks on YouTube or through limited season podcasts. The idea is to create videos with your audiobook as the soundtrack and just a single image or a series of repeating images for the video track. To earn money, they rely on YouTube's advertising policies. You must first gain a certain number of followers and have a certain level of hours played. Check YouTube policies for the current requirements to monetize your channel.

One idea is to call the audiobooks a podcast. If you have a book series, each book in the series is a different season.

Audio-First or Audio-Only. In a reaction to kids reading on or otherwise using computers, there are a couple products that promote "No Screens." The Yoto platform and the Tonie platform are both audio-first or audio-only ways for kids to consume books, podcasts, news, and so on.

The Tonie is a unique audio player that allows customers to purchase a variety of separate audio recordings. They use a plastic character to represent each audio selection. The character is placed on the Tonie device, which triggers the audio. Those characters are expensive to create, so they need lots of sales, which means they rely on branded characters such as Disney characters. Also, they need an hour of content, so picture books rarely work, but chapter books are too long. It's not a great fit for most authors.

Yoto players, from a British company, are also a unique audio player, but they rely on printed cards to trigger the audio. In late 2024, they opened a creator market to selected people, allowing audio creators to publish a wide variety of materials on their platform. However, they request that creators order cards to make available in their stores. I consider this an onerous up-front cost, so I don't currently recommend them. As I write this, though, Yoto's business plan is developing. Check to see if it meets your needs.

Audiobook Files

For audiobooks, you need these files. File names are always ISBN numbers.

- Audiobook cover image files are always a square format, 2400px by 2400px, jpeg format, less than 5MB.
- Audio recordings of the story as .mp4 files, following the specifications discussed above. I usually have an Opening, Main Story and Closing files, numbered as ISBN-1.mp4, ISBN-2.mp4, and ISBN-3.mp4. For novels, you'll number chapters sequentially, too. After you have all the files sequenced, use a standard program to zip the files for delivery.

- Metadata. Most platforms require a spreadsheet for metadata, that will include the narrator's name. Some platforms also want to know the run time of the audiobook expressed as hours:minutes:seconds. For example, an audiobook that is 1 hour, 26 minutes, and 14 seconds long would be 1:26:14 in length.

In the end, you'll have to decide if the audiobook format is worth the time investment for your books.

• • • • • • •

ACTION: Decide if you will offer audiobook formats for your books. Some authors will want to start offering audiobooks right away, but some will want to add them in the future. Decide at what point it makes sense to add audiobooks to your offerings.

Chapter 28
Valuing Your Work

Writing is a strange profession where you sit alone in your cave and work and work, until you finally come out with a finished book. And it's natural to ask, what's the value of this work?

A book isn't complete until it has a reader. But does the reader value your book?

In other words, what will you charge for your book? But beyond that, what will you charge for your related work as an author, such as school visits and public speaking?

How do you value your work?

What will you charge for your books?

For the ebook of your middle-grade novel, should you give it away free or charge $11.99? For the ebook of your picture book, what should you charge? The legacy publishers often price ebooks at $8.99 or upwards. Some say that the market is very tough for hardcover picture books priced over $19.99. Can you charge that and still make a profit?

Let's look at the complicated subject of how to value your work. First, there's the emotional side of value. It's hard because your ego is all wrapped up in your book. But when you start thinking about it, the ugly Imposter Syndrome raises its head. Are you a "real" writer? Is your work of any value to readers? Or is it worthless?

Assigning value to your work can easily become an emotional rollercoaster. You, and only you, understand how much work, love, passion, and time it took to produce the book. But when you release the book, the public will have reactions, both positive and negative. Remember our discussion that you will live or die by your opinion? I encouraged you to listen to your voice and stand up for your vision for your work.

When you price your work, it's another time to embrace your opinions. However, those opinions will now slam up against the realities of the marketplace. To acquire readers and build an audience means the readers must choose your book rather than someone else's book.

Second, your decisions about how to produce certain formats will mean you must cover production costs. For a POD printed book, the costs are highest, while ebook production costs are much lower. How do you sort it all out?

Profit Margins

Here's a general guideline: across all formats, I try to price my books so that I make $2–3/book profit. That is after all the production, marketing, and delivery costs, I work to price so that I have $2–3 profit/book. That's not a random number, but it's based on the SRP, typical POD print costs, typical 55% wholesale discount, and standard accounting. We could work through all the math, but for products below $20–25, it's a good goal.

You should set a Suggested Retail Price (SRP) for each format of your book, which, by law, will be standardized across all sales platforms. Then, each platform has the right to discount or price the book as they need for their business practices. Amazon and Barnes and Noble could each sell the same book, but at different prices. But as a publisher, you quote those stores the same SRP.

To set an SRP, I look at the most expensive production costs. For paperback and hardcover, that is usually IngramSpark, with a wholesale discount set for 55%, no returns. (See more on the issue in Book Returns? Yes or No chapter.)

NOTE: Prices are correct as I write this, but you can check current pricing here: https://myaccount.ingramspark.com/Portal/Tools/PubCompCalculator

For a 32-page, hardcover case (no dust jacket), full-color, standard 70 paper, 8.5″ × 8.5″, print cost of $8.13 and the standard 55% discount.

List price (SRP) - Profit
$19.99 - profit $0.57
$20.99 - profit $1.01
$21.99 - profit $1.44
$22.99 - profit $1.88
$23.99 - profit $2.31
$24.99 - profit $2.75
$25.99 - profit $3.18

NOTE: This is pricing for standard70, which means it is 70 weight paper and standard printing. If you with to use premium printing, the print costs will be higher.

I currently charge $24.99 SRP for my picture books in the hardcover format. When I set that price, I understand that bookstores will be unable to sell the book at that price because they want books under $20. That means my main market is schools, libraries, and individuals. But I must set that SRP on this platform so that I earn a profit of $2 minimum.

If you use a different POD printer, you may be able to calculate a lower pricing, but the SRP still needs to be set for the highest printer. Across platforms, you're expected to have your pricing set to the same SRP. This is also the price that you'll set in any catalog you produce.

However, after you set your SRP—it's just the "suggested" retail price—any platform can set discounts, sale prices, and promotional pricing. If you sell direct at a craft fair, school visit, or on an online store, you can also set a promotional price. This makes sense because each venue or bookstore will expect to price for their customers.

Wholesale customers will be expected to calculate discounts based on the SRP. For example, if you offer a 40% or 50% wholesale discount, the pricing will be calculated on the SRP.

What will you charge for school visits?

When I visit a school, I ask for a reasonable professional fee. I'm losing a day of work; it takes time to prepare a presentation; and, I'm educational, as well as entertaining. If you're just starting out, ask for a modest fee ($100–500). Specify the number of presentations you'll do in a day, typically four, five, or six. That lets the school plan your schedule and the class rotations.

Once your backlist expands and you gain experience in school visits, you can raise your rates. Awards and starred reviews can also add to the perceived value of your work and deserve an increase in rates. One reading teacher told me that if you have a starred review, you shouldn't go anywhere for less than $1000/day. There will be a limit to how much you charge because of the realities of school budgets. Newbery award-winning authors (the highest award for children's literature from the American Library Association) can ask for $3000/day and up, so that's the practical upper limit of school visit fees.

Do take the time to develop a good presentation, because your reputation—and future school visits—will depend on how well you deliver. And develop a handout to send home for parents to purchase signed copies of your books.

To find schools that book authors and learn more about school visits, look for Facebook groups that focus on school visits.

What will you charge for keynoting, teaching, or other speaking?

If you're asked to teach writing, speak about great books for kids, do motivational speeches, or other public speaking opportunities, do not sell yourself short. You've written and published a great book. That is a huge accomplishment. Of course, at the beginning of your career, speaking fees are lower. Often an organization has budgeted a certain honorarium and can't exceed that. But sometimes, the fees are negotiable. Negotiate.

What is your reputation?

Finally, what is your reputation worth?

When I started working on *Be Strong: The Rise of Beloved Public Art Sculptor Nancy Schön*, one person asked, "Why would Nancy work with you on her biography?"

Nancy is famous for creating the Boston Public Garden duck sculpture based on *Make Way for Ducklings* by Robert McCloskey. The questioner was really asking about my reputation. Was I a nobody, or did I have the "right" to ask a famous person if I could work on her biography?

We are NOT nobodies. After successfully publishing 70+ books, winning awards for science, history, and language arts, I am not nobody. My reputation for great books means I can approach any topic I like.

Furthermore, I don't shy away from asking for interviews. I've interviewed the scientist for live animal experiments on the International Space Station, the biologist at the Papahānaumokuākea

Marine National Monument on Midway Island, the herpetologist in charge of 40 years of tortoise restoration in the Galapagos Islands, Brazilian puma scientists, frog jockeys who jump bullfrogs in the Calaveras County contests, scientists at the Prague Zoo and the Denver Zoo, and much more. Their work and lives are fascinating and provide background and vital information for my nonfiction work.

Build your reputation by writing and publishing amazing books. Then build on that reputation to write something even more amazing!

• • • • • • •

ACTION: Based on typical specs for a book you plan to offer and the printers you plan to use, decide on a Suggested Retail Price. Be sure to check each platform to make sure you're making $2-3/book sale.

If you plan to do school visits, decide on your professional speaking fee. For example, you may decide on a fee of $450 for up to four presentations/day.

Chapter 29
Book Returns? Yes or no?

You're about to learn something about yourself! How do you deal with risks? Are you risk-averse or are you comfortable taking risks?

When you set up a book with IngramSpark, you are asked if you will accept returns. What does this mean and what should you answer?

To understand the issue, we should go back to the Great Depression of the 1930s in the United States. To help bookstores survive the desperate times, publishers offered to take returns on unsold books. This developed over time into a standard practice. Sometimes, paperback books weren't actually returned; instead, the bookstore stripped off the front covers which were returned to the publisher as proof the store had stocked the books for a while. It was more expensive to actually ship the paperback books back to the publisher. But the practice of taking returns has never gone away.

In some ways, it makes sense because if a 2023 title isn't selling, wouldn't you rather use that book shelf space for a 2025 book that "might" sell better? You can also see, though, how that mentality would start to favor new titles over the backlist. It developed into a system of "new is good." Or, as Dean Wesley Smith has put it, under this type system, your books "spoil" quickly, just like produce. You must have fresh fruits and vegetables to stock the shelves.

Enter Print-on-Demand (POD) in the late 1990s and into the early 2000s. The old method of offset printing is now referred to as Print-First-Sell-Later. You print a large number of books at low cost per unit, then sell them. POD is a Sell-First-Print-Later approach. When you have an order in hand, then you print. The initial investment is only the illustrations, layout and design, copyediting, and marketing. It's a very different business model.

But when the POD business model collides with the standard practices of bookstores, we run into the question of taking returns. Independent bookstores are also a small business and run on very tight margins. If they have to keep stock indefinitely, it means they can't stock the newest titles and potentially lose sales. They passionately protect this right to return books that don't sell. From their point of view, it makes sense. If you want to sell to physical bookstores, you must consider this issue carefully.

Independent bookstores have also worked hard in the last ten or fifteen years to manage their stock more wisely. With just-in-time ordering and shipping, they order smaller quantities, but reorder more often.

It's estimated that front list titles will run 25% returns and backlist will have 15% returns. In a controversial move in 2024, Barnes & Noble cut back on stocking hardcover middle-grade novels because the return rate was running 80% or more. However, I've seen reports that independent bookstores strive for more like 8% returns. My experience has been 0% to 1% on some titles. In other words, your returns rate can vary by genre, format, and specific title. The only way to know is to test it.

Let's look at the issue in more depth.

Taking Returns - 3 Questions to Ask

The question of taking returns usually refers to orders from book-stores, so the first question to ask is this:

Are bookstores your main market?

For many authors today, their main markets are online sales on Amazon or ebook platforms. Physical bookstores are a low priority market for them. Perhaps, as a children's book author, your main markets are school visits or other educational market opportunities.

Do you care about bookstore sales? I know there's a certain nostalgia to thinking that your books are available in your local book-store. And certainly, if you use Ingram Spark as your POD printer, it's possible.

But is it your main market? I've found that I'm comfortable saying, "I don't care about bookstore sales. My main markets are schools and libraries."

A second question is what kind of financial shape are you in? Do you have a reserve of cash? If you are suddenly hit with a big return bill, can you absorb that loss and still function? If you have no cash reserves, it's very risky to accept returns. With a larger cash reserve, you may wish to test the waters to see if accepting returns will mean that bookstores will carry your books.

A final question is how risk-averse are you? When you accept returns, you don't know if a sale is complete for 180 days because the store can return the book(s) anytime up to 180 days. Let's say you sold $1,000 of books. Your account is credited and you receive a payment for $1,000. But at the end of 180 days, the book-store returns $900 worth of books. At that point, the POD company will hand you a bill for that $900! You must return the money.

You must also decide what to do with the returned books. You can choose to also have the books shipped to you at your expense, or destroyed. Consider first that shipping charge. Then, if you have the books shipped to you, you can resell them—if they are in good shape. Often, they are shop-worn with dings here and there, making reselling hard. They may only be good for donating to a charitable cause, or giveaways at a teacher conference. It's heartbreaking to destroy printed books, but sometimes, it's the best financial decision to just take a small loss rather than a larger loss.

Taking returns is not a straightforward yes or no answer because it depends on how well you tolerate risk. I've decided that I'm risk-averse. I can't bring myself to accept returns.

Take Returns? Pros

The biggest advantage to taking returns is you have access to the wider physical-bookstore market. Your book, at least the first six months of launching, can easily be stocked on bookstores across the U.S.

If you ask for returned copies to be sent back to you, the cost will include shipping so your costs for that title are high; however, you have the opportunity to resell it, assuming it's in good shape.

Take Returns? Cons

A sale isn't final for 180 days. You may be paid by the POD company in 60 or 90 days, but that money is still at risk until the returns period is over. Therefore, carefully read the policy for any POD company you deal with.

Taking Returns - Options

A final consideration is that most POD printers allow you to change the returns status whenever you want. One idea is to leave a book eligible for returns for the first six months after publication. Bookstores are more likely to stock a new book, so it makes sense. You'd get access to bookstores initially. If sales are strong, you can monitor the return rate and when sales start to drop and returns rise, then switch to a NO RETURNS status. In this case, you'd keep most backlist titles at NO RETURNS.

OR, some reports say that returns are lower on backlist titles. You may choose to accept returns on backlist, but not on front list.

OR, some reports say that hardcover middle grade novels are the hardest to sell in a bookstore. You might decide to put those titles at NO RETURNS, but for paperback nonfiction titles, you would accept returns.

In other words, you can develop a policy of returns that works for you, your books, and your goals for placing books in certain places to encourage sales. And you can change it when your business changes, whenever you want.

Always, though, consider that third question: how healthy are your finances? In the early days of your career, when you only have a few books, you may not want to consider returns at all because you can't afford a huge hit. As your backlist and your income grow, it may be worth the expanded market sometimes. For certain time periods. Or for certain books.

• • • • • • •

ACTION: Write the answer to these questions:

How risk-averse are you? Will you take returns? When? What returns strategy makes sense for your publishing program?

Part Five
Marketing Pre-Publication

Your marketing efforts will always depend on where your book falls on the marketing timeline. Is it pre-publication, launch, or post-launch? Overwhelmingly, you must set up the book for success in the pre-publication phase. From metadata to preorders, success starts here.

During the pre-publication phase, before a book ever comes out, there are crucial tasks to ensure the book's success: correct metadata, review copies and reviews, newsletters, preorders, and catalogs. Let's get to it!

Chapter 30
Distribution

Distribution must be in place before you start any promotions or marketing. Can you imagine spending $1,000 in advertising, but when the reader gets to their favorite online store, your book is not available?

A disaster.

Developing distribution in a wide number of places is crucial because it provides multiple income streams. It means you're not dependent on one company for all your income, a smart business decision.

So, where can readers find your books?

Readers need to find your books where *they* want to find your books. If they consistently buy or consume books from certain channels, they will continue to look for books on those channels. They will only rarely move to another channel to buy or consume a book.

We know that only about 20 percent of people buy new books[1], while the rest find books in the library, from friends, or from a used bookstore. So, you need to consider where your readers buy books, but also whether they check out audiobooks or ebooks on a library app, like the Libby App from Overdrive. Where else would people find your books, in any format, that could produce an income stream?

Major Distributors

There's no reason to limit your book sales to a small locality. Instead, you can distribute worldwide through several means. Here's a list, which is not exhaustive; look for other options that will fit your books, especially because these options will change over time.

Print (hardcover and/or paperback) Distribution

- IngramSpark POD account. Your book is added to its sister company, Ingram Wholesale, catalog, which makes it available worldwide.
- Amazon through a POD account with KDP. Your book is automatically added to Amazon.com and all international Amazon platforms. Do NOT enable Extended Distribution because that just sends it to Ingram Wholesale, but at a lower percentage rate. I recommend setting up books on both IngramSpark and KDP.
- Shopify store powered by Lulu Direct POD printing. Do not use Lulu distribution because the extra fees make it unprofitable.

Ebook Distribution

- Amazon's KDP account. Use the same KDP account to set up paper and ebooks. See the "KU or Wide?" chapter for more on ebook options here.
- Apple iTunes.
- GooglePlay
- Kobo Writing Life

eBook Aggregators

- Draft2Digital
- PublishDrive

Reading Apps for ebooks

- EPIC!
- Booka
- Amazon/KDP's Kindle Unlimited, requires exclusive on ebooks

Audiobooks

- Spotify for Authors
- Apple iTunes
- GooglePlay
- ACX, Amazon's platform for audiobooks
- EPIC! App adds audio to create read-to-me versions of the ebook, a popular option on the platform.

This book isn't an exhaustive explanation of any particular platform, and I urge you to investigate the best options for your books. Each of the major distributors has pros and cons, so look for a balanced discussion of the platforms. When you're first starting, I recommend Amazon's KDP platform, but after mastering that, you should expand into other distribution methods.

What Are Your Wholesale Terms?

When you provide books to retailers, you are acting as a wholesaler, which means you'll need to discount your books so they can mark up the book and make a profit. You need to develop your policies for working with other retailers as a wholesaler, such as schools, gift shops, museums, and other retail outlets.

When you POD with Ingram or KDP, the wholesale pricing is built into the dashboard. On KDP, the percentages are set, and on the pricing page, you'll just see the List Price, List Price with VAT (international taxes), Print Cost, Royalty Rate, and Royalty. You cannot change the royalty rate of 60 percent on print books. On ebooks, you can change from 35 percent to 70 percent. Amazon charges delivery fees for ebooks, which is negligible for novels, but can add up quickly for full-color picture books. If your file sizes are over 8MB, you can switch to 35 percent royalty, which does NOT charge delivery fees. For more, see the "Creating ePubs for Kindle" chapter.

On IngramSpark, you must set up wholesale discount percentages. That is, you will have a Suggested Retail Price (SRP) and a Wholesale price that is a percentage of the SRP. Usually, Ingram recommends the industry-standard 55 percent discount. If your book sells for $10, that means you sell it to a retail vendor for $4.50, from which you must subtract the print cost to find your profit. You should adjust your list price and discount percentages to receive the profit you want. Read the "Book Returns? Yes or No" chapter for more information on setting up wholesale pricing on IngramSpark.

Other distributors have negotiable terms. You'll need to calculate your profit margins and decide on policies for your store.

Example 1: You give a 40 percent discount, but free shipping.

Example 2: You give a 50 percent discount, but the buyer must pay for shipping.

Whatever your policy, it's a good idea to create a webpage (See: https://mimshousebooks.com/pages/wholesale) and/or a PDF wholesale handout with your policies. Include your logo, address, phone number, email, discount rate, policy on shipping, return policy, and payment options. I recommend you accept credit card payment before shipping, but you may offer net-30, which is payment in 30 days. Include your wholesale policy with your catalog or any marketing material you send to retail customers.

Educational Distributors

Educational distributors are local, regional, or national companies who develop relationships with schools and educators to provide books. They specialize in finding great prices for books needed locally or for special educational programs. For example, they may work with a school committee to develop a reading list for a project, then source the books.

If you publish with IngramSpark, your books are probably listed in their catalog. However, sometimes—for large orders—they may contact you directly for a quote on a bulk purchase. Generally, they want great terms to make their efforts worthwhile. 50 percent discount is a minimum, but they often prefer deeper discounts. Shipping is negotiable. I've had sales of 1,400 books, 900 books, or just 15 books from such companies. So, I try to work with them when it makes sense.

When I get a request for information, I send them to my wholesale webpage and/or send them the wholesale terms PDF. I love it when they want a lot of books AND give me a lead time of 3–4 months. With that, I go to an offset printer to get better print costs and better profits. If I only have a couple weeks, I'll choose whichever POD print company has the best prices and shipping. Ingram allows for direct shipping, but their prices are higher so they usually don't get these orders. LuluDirect has great quality for picture books so I use them often. Or, if I have orders from Hawaii, I usually order author copies from Amazon because their shipping is so reasonable—and more reliable.

Penguin Random House often lists online the educational distributors[2] who carry their books. Look for an updated list as a place to start. I've sold through at least six different educational distributors. You should investigate each company to see if it is right for your books and your catalog. I contact these companies and provide an updated catalog and ask about opportunities to work together.

Educational Book Fairs

Educational book fairs are one of the toughest markets to conquer, but we know that it's where kids buy tons of books! Because the book fairs are in the schools, promoted by the teachers or librarians, and often offer low-priced books, it's a place where kids buy books. And when grandparents are invited to attend a book fair with their grand-kids—lots of books can sell.

Scholastic Book Fairs, the biggest and oldest of the fairs, are virtually closed to indie publishers. Legacy publishers are invited to pitch books and the competition is fierce. Scholastic works hard to curate a book list that will sell and earn a profit. Sometimes, you may be able to get local interest books accepted through your local Scholastic Book Fair personnel, but even that can be hard.

Literati Book Fairs, out of Austin, TX—which began as Follett Book Fairs before Literati bought it—is also hard to crack. At one point, they had a Google form to submit books. I thought I'd have a chance with *A Little Bit of Dinosaur* because it had 6 million reads on EPIC!, a starred Kirkus Review, and several science awards. The rejection note did say it was a cute book, but ended with the dreaded "but it doesn't meet our current needs" comment.

Indie authors can't get into Scholastic, but what if we could use other smaller book fair companies? Regional book fairs, religious book fairs, or other specialized book fairs can be popular for some schools. In general, it's a difficult and bleak market. The terms are often onerous and don't work for my print-on-demand business model.

For example, I've seen terms like this: 65 percent discount, publisher pays shipping, and unsold books are returnable at the end of the season. I usually offer 50 percent discount (or 55 percent for large orders). I can't accept returns, and shipping costs are rising so that I rarely offer free shipping anymore.

So, some small, regional, or genre-focused book fairs look good until you see their terms. To sell books cheaply, the book fair companies need such deals though.

In general, then, educational book fairs are a low-budget, bottom-dollar market with fierce competition. The payoffs can be huge because of volume sales, but my business plan doesn't let me pursue this distribution market. I'm still open to discussions, of course, and perhaps someday it will happen. Just not yet.

Libraries

While there are several ways to approach libraries about your books (book launch party, author visit, etc.), I'll focus here on getting your books on their shelves or virtual shelves.

One of my major distribution points for libraries is ebooks and audiobooks through Overdrive. They use the Libby App for corporate, academic, or private libraries, and the Sora app for school libraries. Apply to go direct here: https://company.overdrive.com/publishers/

The first time I applied, I was rejected. But a couple months later, they invited me. Probably a library was looking for my books, which is one big tip: when a patron asks for your book at their library, it's more likely to be purchased. Ask your fans to ask their libraries to carry your book!

Going direct has its pros and cons. To submit books, you upload the book files and spreadsheets with the metadata for your books. Or you can use ONIX, the book industry standard for transporting metadata; it's hard to use and not for the faint-hearted.

Overdrive does provide dedicated reps for small publishers who will advocate for your books. I've found their effectiveness to be uneven, with better sales one year, but not the next. Still, they are aware that small publishers have different needs.

If you don't want to go direct or aren't accepted, you can access Overdrive through Draft2Digital; this method means you give D2D a percentage, and while they do give you access to Overdrive sales promotions, it's often limited to only a couple titles.

For print books in libraries, the best tip is again to ask your fans to ask the library to buy the book. I've been told again and again that librarians try to respond to patron requests. Librarians still care about reviews in respected journals, so work to get those. Make sure your books are available, which means they are listed in Ingram Wholesale through IngramSpark so they can be ordered easily. Hardcovers are preferred for the library market.

Gift Shops

Selling wholesale to gift shops or other small venues is another distribution option. The Boston Tea Party Gift Shop in Boston has been carrying my historical title, *George Washington's Engineer: How Rufus Putnam Won the Siege of Boston without Firing a Shot.* They weren't interested in any other titles, because they have such a tight focus on U.S. Colonial history.

But that's the way of gift shops; they often have a special focus. Perhaps it's a local focus, and you'll be welcomed as a local author. Or, a STEM toy shop might be interested in your STEM books.

In other words, selling to gift shops can and does work, but it's a one-by-one sale. You'll need to work to develop relationships at multiple shops and keep them informed of your books. After an initial contact, I send them to my wholesale page and my catalog page. When my catalog updates, I try to send to all such customers.

There are online wholesale markets to make this easy. As a trial, I listed books on Faire.com for six months—with zero sales. But your experience may vary, and there are new marketplaces coming online all the time. Be sure to investigate terms before you sign up and give a new platform at least six months to build.

For more on selling wholesale, see the Wholesale in a Box blog. It's a great resource.

Attending Craft Shows or Other Local Opportunities

Some authors and illustrators love going to local shows and setting up a table or booth. I know authors who have a regular circuit of shows, and their lifestyle is traveling to these shows. To make this work, you'll likely need offset printed books so you can give discounted pricing to attendees at a show.

Work to develop an appealing display at your table or booth. You'll need racks or boxes to provide multiple visual levels. Here's where you may also sell plush animals, stickers, temporary tattoos, or other small toys—under $5–10 items are "throw-away gifts," or impulse buys that parents will buy for kids, which add to your bottom line.

Full-Service Distribution

Another distribution option is to move to a full-service distributor. This would be a total change of your business plan because they require stock for each title. You'd have to offset-print books, ship to the distributor's warehouse, and keep track of inventory. POD is a sell-first, print-later business model. Full-service distribution is a print-first, sell-later business model.

Many places that sell books require a full-service distributor who can deal with pallets of books. For example, Bass Pro Shops might sell thousands of copies of a picture book about a father-son going fishing together. Their orders can be huge! But they require specific shipping capabilities, such as delivery of pallets, so they only deal with established distributors.

Full-service distributors prefer publishers to be earning at least $50,000/year. Simon and Schuster has a distribution program for small publishers. See more at https://www.simonandschusterpublishing.com/sns-distribution/

Keeping the Distribution Strong

When a distribution partner (a gift shop or museum, for example) is doing well selling my books, and there's a strong communication channel (sadly, not always available), then I make sure they get updates about my books. I send my seasonal catalog, notes about awards, and updates on discounts or sales. Keeping the relationship working is important and requires work! But it's vitally important.

Curating Your Distributors

Every year, I add new distributors and drop off those that perform poorly for my books. It makes sense! For my sanity—since I am accounting-challenged—I want distributors that bring in at least $1,000/year. If they don't, then I look for ways to continue the relationship, but lessen the time commitment. For example, Apple ebooks and Kobo ebooks are not strong markets for my curriculum-related picture books. A couple years ago, I moved my ebooks to Draft2Digital, an ebook aggregator. The books are still available on Apple and Kobo, but I don't have to spend valuable time updating them.

Where else could you find readers for your books? Work to find distributors that make sense for your books. Lift up your eyes! Books are sold all around you, in many venues and markets. One of them might be your most profitable market.

• • • • • • •

ACTION: Decide on your basic distributors and create accounts or apply for accounts. I recommend you start with KDP and Ingram. Then do a yearly review of your distributors and expand as it seems reasonable.

Chapter 31
Metadata

Before a book ever comes out, there are crucial tasks to ensure its success: correct metadata, review copies and reviews, newsletters, preorders, and catalogs.

Metadata: Make Sure Your Book Is Findable

When you put a book for sale online, it's vital that people can search and find your book. Everything online works with search engines. So, what's the secret of making your book findable? Great metadata!

Metadata is the data about your book: title, subtitle, categories, ISBN, CIP data, cover photo, description, keywords, and so on.

If you're indie published, when you created your copyright page, you already decided on categories, ISBN, and CIP data. If you're legacy published, then the publisher decided all of that.

Metadata is grouped into these basic data points:

- ISBN
- Title

- Format or Binding
- Publication Date
- BISAC Subject Code
- Retail Price
- Sales Rights
- Cover image
- Contributor(s)

How Important is Metadata?

According to the 2021 Nielsen publication, *The Importance of Metadata for Discoverability and Sales* report[1], titles with complete metadata average twice the sales (110% more) than those with incomplete metadata. When this information was provided at least 16 weeks before publication, sales were 44% higher.

They studied the importance of each piece of data, looking at sales figures when the data is present or missing.

- **Cover image**: 94% higher sales
- **BISAC code**: 268% higher sales
- **Keywords**: 140% higher sales
- **Descriptive elements**: Long description--144% higher sales (500+ words recommended)
- **Short description**: 4% higher sales
- **Author biography**: 97% higher sales
- **Reviews**: 83% higher sales
- **Overall**: Complete metadata resulted in three times as many sales.
- **Libraries**: Books with complete metadata have double borrows in libraries.

CIP - Cataloguing in Publication
The CIP data is a bunch of data on the copyright page that tells

librarians how to catalog your book. One librarian said, "Without a CIP block, the book looks naked."

That's why I pay attention to this block of information: librarians care about it, and they are my audience.

CIP is a program administered by the Library of Congress. Here's how they describe it:

"A Cataloging in Publication record (aka CIP data) is a bibliographic record prepared by the Library of Congress for a book that has not yet been published. When the book is published, the publisher includes the CIP data on the copyright page thereby facilitating book processing for libraries and book dealers."

Large publishers use the CIP, but for small and indie-publisher, there's a work-around, the PCN, or Preassigned Control Number. The LOC explains the difference in the CIP and PCN programs:

"The Cataloging in Publication (CIP) program creates bibliographic records for forthcoming books most likely to be widely acquired by U.S. libraries. The Preassigned Control Number (PCN) program assigns a Library of Congress Control Number to titles most likely to be acquired by the Library of Congress as well as some other categories of books. The two programs are mutually exclusive."

On a practical level, this means that a couple months before I publish a children's book, I request a PCN (https://www.loc.gov/programs/preassigned-control-number/about-this-program/)

Usually, they are fast, answering with a day or so. Just click on "Open an Account," and follow directions.

OK. So you get the PCN number. So what? The PCN number should be placed on the copyright page. But you should take it a step farther and get the CIP data block. This is the CIP block for my book, NEFERTIT, THE SPIDERNAUT, which came out in October, 2016:

Publisher's Cataloging-in-Publication data

Names: Pattison, Darcy, author. | Tisnés, Valeria, illustrator. Title: Nefertiti , the spidernaut : the jumping spider who learned to hunt in space / By Darcy Pattison ; Illustrated by Valeria Tisnés. Description: Little Rock, Arkansas: Mim's House, 2016. Identifiers: ISBN 9781629440606 (Hardcover) | 9781629440613 (pbk.) | 9781629440620 (ebook) | LCCN 2015920985. Summary: A jumping spider is sent to the International Space Station to discover if she can hunt in microgravity. Subjects: LCSH Space biology --Juvenile literature. | Animal experimentation --Juvenile literature. | International Space Station -- Research --Juvenile literature. | Space stations--Juvenile literature. | Space flight--Physiological effect --Juvenile literature. | Jumping spiders--Juvenile literature. | BISAC JUVENILE NONFICTION / Animals / Insects, Spiders, etc. | JUVENILE NONFICTION / Technology / Aeronautics, Astronautics & Space Science. Classification: LCC QH327 .P38 2016 | DDC 629.45009 --dc23

Or look at the CIP Block on the copyright page of this book.

Does this look complicated? It does to me, too. I tried for a while to learn the intricacies of this info, but found it an unreasonable time drain. It's one of the things I always find a freelancer for. You can ask a local librarian if they could do it. But I like to use Adrienne Bashista, Cataloguer-at-Large, (CIPBlock.com) because she's reasonably priced, keeps up-to-date on changes in the CIP requirements, and is relatively fast. I'm not an affiliate or anything, just a satisfied customer.

The final step is to be sure to send a copy of your book to the LOC when it becomes available. That completes the registration for the CIP. When I file my copyright (http://www.copyright.gov/eco/) I send the book at the same time.

Will this help sell your book? Maybe, maybe not. I know that librarians are much more comfortable placing my book into their school library when this information is present on the copyright page. It's a small expense and well worth it to me.

KEYWORDS

Keywords should add descriptive data that helps a title's discoverability when searched for. Some platforms, such as GooglePlay, allow you to add a list of words at the bottom of the description. Most, however, prefer that the keywords are integrated into the description in a natural way.

Include:

- Character names and geographical locations.
- Broad terms that help a reader understand the book's content.
- Themes of the book, such as grief, competition, or friendship.
- Related books by the author. Example: For 10-14 year old readers, a story of friendship unfolds in this cozy mystery, set in the Appalachian Mountains. By the author of *Mountain Man Mystery: A Cozy Mystery*.

Experts recommend that you use unique, consumer-oriented, relevant keywords. But not obscure keywords that no one will search for. One interesting way to research keywords is Google Trends, a free service. For example, if you have a science-related picture book, it's clear that STEM is the keyword you want.

Most platforms require a semicolon between keywords, but sometimes they ask for a comma.

KEYWORDS ON AMAZON.COM

On KDP, seven keywords are allowed, with up to 500 characters. Most recommend that you fill up the entire space.

1. Use jargon, anything new, distinctive, or specific. Ex. Baseball grand slam.
2. When the reader doesn't know the exact title or author, AND the title may be very different from the theme, then use keywords that relate to the title, theme, and author.
3. Use generic terms for the topic. Broader descriptive terms where the title may straddle more than one classification.
4. Don't repeat the BISAC or category codes, but include the topic if it's worded slightly different.
5. If more than one topic is included in the book, add those in the keywords.
6. Use common synonyms of the BISAC category.
7. Use commonly known subject terms not referred to anywhere else in the metadata.
8. Include specific names of characters, fictional places, or series names that may not be anywhere else in the metadata.
9. Use titles of related books in a series or related author.
10. Include any concept or theme that the reader may include or exclude from the search.
11. Use additional titles in an anthology, box set, or book of short stories.
12. Identify the publication year of annual publication.

13. To indicate audience, especially when someone not from that audience may be searching for it. Ex. Gift for grads, mother's day gift

RESOURCES

Chesson, Dave: Amazon Keyword Rules: New Update. June 2024. https://youtu.be/4oYxlvuTcXQ?si=v8UjlaJHvlQHmkZn

   Look for other updates from Kindlepreneur/Dave Chesson, who keeps a sharp eye on changes at KDP.

Lexile Scores

For school markets, you need one more metadata statistic: what is your book's reading level? The education world relies on Lexile scores from Metametrics, Inc. (https://metametricsinc.com/content-measurement/) For small publishers, they offer à la carte pricing. If you market to schools, teachers and librarians will appreciate this information.

Amazon's AuthorCentral

Once you've set up books on KDP, you should sign up for access to your book's information on AuthorCentral at author.amazon.com. Here, you'll be able to claim books and then see metadata, reviews, sales rank on Amazon, access to advertising, various other reports, and your profile on Amazon. Be sure to set up the profile as desired so it provides readers with information. Remember—you want them to know your name! It's great to have one centralized location for information on all your books on the Amazon platform.

Managing Metadata

When you create metadata (write that description and so on), you need to store it somewhere. Each platform needs the data and it should be consistent across platforms.

The task of maintaining, providing, and updating metadata can eat up your time. You must find a way to deal with it efficiently. If you only have a couple titles, a spreadsheet is fine. Each partner will have their own proprietary template for metadata. You'll find yourself cutting and pasting data as you upload to different partners. If you have over twenty titles, it may be worth setting up a small database, such as Microsoft's Access database program.

When your backlist fills out with 50+ titles, you may consider setting up ONIX for your titles. This is the industry standard system of providing book information to vendors and providers. However, it's difficult to learn and master. Currently, the best option is OnixEdit.-com, which offers a Cloud Subscription. For more robust ONIX feeds, look at Eloquence on Demand from FirebrandTech.com.

Create a Sell Sheet for each book

For each book, I create a one- or two-page sell sheet that includes all the metadata. Include company information, all the book's metadata, including bios of authors or illustrators, and keep it updated when reviews come in or the author or illustrator have updated bios. When you send out review copies, include this, along with a catalog, if available.

• • • • • • •

ACTION: Decide if you will use the CIP data in your books and how you will obtain that block of data.

If you plan to use CIP, set up an an account for the PCN program: https://www.loc.gov/programs/preassigned-control-number/about-this-program/

Decide if you will obtain Lexile scores for your books. If you wish to use these reading scores, contact Metametrics for more information.

Set up an account at Amazon's AuthorCentral, and optimize your information.

Decide how you will set up and maintain your books' metadata. I recommend starting with a simple spreadsheet. Set it up and use it for your first book and revise as needed for subsequent books.

Chapter 32
Fan-Loyalty

W hen I first started researching self-publishing, I read Peter Bowerman's book, *The Well-Fed Self-Publisher*. He said one thing that has stuck with me:

"...you have one job and only one job: build the demand for your book." —Peter Bowerman

---

Recently, I've been reading Peter Hildick-Smith, whose company Codex Group researches for the legacy publishers, on the impact of an author's reputation. Jane Friedman interviewed him in a 2023 Hot Sheet newsletter article.[1]

Hildick-Smith asks, "What does an author bring to the table and how does it affect sales?"

Essentially, he says the same thing as Bowerman:

What matters is the demand for the author's next book. —Peter
Hildick-Smith

Do you recognize the author's name? Do you know enough about
their work that you want to read their next book? Or is the topic of
their book of interest?

It's clear that the main driver of big sales is fan loyalty.

For example, when J. K. Rowling, author of the Harry Potter
series, published an adult mystery/thriller book under the pen name
Robert Galbraith, it did poorly. But when the newspapers reported
that she wrote the book, sales soared. The difference? Her name.

Hildick-Smith reported that fans have an average probability of
40% of wanting to buy an author's next book after discovering it. That
drops to 10% or less when the book reader is only casually familiar
with the author. We need that name recognition!

However, it's important to say that name recognition alone isn't
enough. Hildick-Smith measured the name recognition of Colleen
Hoover early in her TikTok success. Hoover took TikTok by storm in
2021 to 2023, resulting in her book, *It Ends with Us*, as #1 on the
New York Times bestseller list and giving Hoover thriving career
with millions of book sales. Early on, fans didn't know her name; that
is, they knew the TikTok influencers' names, and on the basis of their
recommendation, readers bought books. Eventually, when Hildick-
Smith retested, though, Hoover's name recognition had soared, and
that helps her to continue to sell books.

"It's hard to form a loyalty to an author if you don't even know
their name." —Peter Hildick-Smith

Hildick-Smith also comments that some well-known celebrities try to sell books, but they aren't known for books, and therefore, sales are poor. About 20% of the U.S. population are book buyers, and the celebrity's audience didn't intersect with that group.

What's needed is name recognition PLUS an audience who buys books. All of this means that your marketing should focus on finding your audience, making sure the right people read your books and remember your name, and the right people tell others about the books and your name.

Book Title and Subtitle

Here we are at metadata again. Peter Hildick-Smith says the title and subtitle have the potential to draw in readers with intrigue, interest, and curiosity. The goal is to get them to investigate more.

"... the most important initial thing to communicate and motivate demand for a book turns out to be its title—those two or three words—paired with a powerful subtitle. If you don't have enough instant intrigue, interest, and curiosity from that quick, two-second flash of title and cover, what else will start the book shopper on their short journey to get truly motivated to make an actual book purchase?"

Build on Your Success

Hildick-Smith also recommends that you blatantly tie in a bestseller to the next book. If your book, XXX, becomes a bestseller, on the cover of your next book, use the phrase, "by the author of XXX."

Once you've built success for one book, transfer it to the next.

The Goal of Your Marketing Spend: Find Your Audience

My recommendation, then, is to first become a great writer. Your marketing spend at first should be on writing classes that help you become the best writer you can be. Because without a great book, there will never be great fans.

Next, figure out your audience. I hate all the advice that says to build a "persona," a fake person who represents your audience. It all seems fake to me. But there's something to the idea that we may not know our actual audience. Hildick-Smith once worked for a publisher of college textbooks. He asked the question: was their audience college students or college professors? Their research revealed that the college professor was the deciding factor. If a professor chose a book as a textbook for their class, then students bought the book. After that, the publisher focused on marketing to the professors, offering free review samples and other methods. When a professor adopted a class book, it meant big sales. Overall, the publisher sold 10% more books.

Who Is Your Audience? Study Them!

As children's book authors, we know that kids are our first audience. About half of the Alpha generation have access to a debit card or other payment systems, with a monthly allowance of $25–65.[2]

But mostly, our audience is teachers, school librarians, parents, grandparents, or some subset of those. Who is the audience for your books?

When you're thinking about where to spend your marketing dollars this is crucial. My audience is teachers and librarians. Because of that, I know that bookstores are a poor market for me. Instead, I need to understand the educational distributors.

What's important to my audience of teachers and librarians? They still care about reviews, awards from teacher organizations, and of course, word of mouth.

Therefore—because my audience is teachers and librarians—I send all my books for reviews to *School Library Journal*, *Booklist Online*, and I pay for *Kirkus Reviews* (because it's the only place I can reliably and consistently get a review). That is, my first goal in spending marketing dollars is to increase the value of my books by getting a favorable review. Once I get a review, I use it to give teachers/librarians the right information at the right time. Before COVID, that meant I sent out lots of review copies; I'll still do that for selected books. Or, it might mean speaking at local, regional, or national conferences such as the American Library Association or the National Science Teacher's Association. I watch for calls for proposals to speak at such places.

Therefore—because my audience is teachers and librarians—I care about the awards from the teacher organizations: National Science Teacher's Association, National Social Studies Teachers, National Council of Teachers of English, and the National Council of Teachers of Mathematics. And any of the awards that surround the school curriculum: Bank Street College book awards, Reading Council awards from various states, the Texas Bluebonnet award and other state awards, etc. That's why my publishing house, Mims House Books, is a member of the Children's Book Council, because the CBC administers many such awards.

If you're just starting, do school visits. Spend the marketing money on postcards to send to schools, or spend your marketing time in locating and contacting schools for visits. This will enable you to sit and talk with educators. The interaction with kids is extremely valuable, but the downtime between sessions is your chance to pick the brains of the educator.

I ask educators questions: Where do they buy books? Do they only buy rebound books from Follett or Bound-to-Stay-Bound? Or do they buy on Amazon? Where does the school district have accounts that makes it easy for them to buy? And so on...

Capture Your Audience

Whenever possible, capture your audience with signups for a mailing list. (See more in the Newsletter chapter.) Your goal is to develop a back and forth communication. The other problem with marketing books is discoverability. How will fans or casual readers learn about your book? If you have their email and permission to email them, you have gold!

Work to build your reputation. Hildick-Smith says to stop posting about your cat because you're building the wrong audience. Cat lovers may or may not be book buyers!

Instead, talk about books. Your books! What are you working on? Do cover reveals, report on story progress, let them know when or where you'll be speaking, or any of the other things about your career as a book writer.

• • • • • • •

ACTION: Decide who is your main audience: bookstores, parents, school librarians, or the kids themselves. Based on this information, review your target persona, book descriptions (metadata), your targeted distributors, and your marketing plan. Adjust as needed.

Chapter 33
Word of Mouth

W hat is the secret of marketing? Word of Mouth.
On every survey ever done, the #1 reason people buy books is because someone enthusiastically told them about the book. Word of mouth is the best non-secret way to sell books. We know what we need to do! Just inspire people to talk about your books.

The problem, of course, comes down to how to encourage word-of-mouth (WOM)? It's like asking how to create a viral video. The answers aren't straight-forward. Write an amazing book is the short answer. But good books get ignored all the time because no one knows about them. So, after you write that great book, you have to find ways to enter the ongoing conversation about literature. Let's look at marketing activities through the lens of WOM.

What Makes Something Remarkable?

The first thing required for WOM is that there is something to talk about, something to remark upon. For your book, what could someone make remarks about? You can control the conversation when you give them something to talk about.

Appropriate Humor. Top of the list of desirable attributes is humor. Add it to your story first, and then to your marketing.

Controversial - Shock. We remember controversial attitudes! Either side of an issue can provoke engagement. Be careful here, though, or you could make enemies.

Feel Good About Themselves. When people read a story, they are self-centered. It's all about them. Is there something that will make them feel good about themselves? After reading your story, could they say, "I'm a good parent." Or, "I have good taste in toys, especially board games." And so on.

Eye-Catching. Flashy visuals have potential to up the WOM factor. One image going around is of AI-generated fake baby peacocks. Eye-candy! Add some flare to your visuals when possible.

Connection. If you build connection points into your story, ways that people can relate, you'll create WOM. Make them cry. Make them laugh. Make them remember a poignant time of their life. Connect. And WOM will follow.

Timely. Yes, it's good to pay attention to current events and play off them whenever possible. One of my favorite marketing techniques is to play off important dates: holidays, birthdays, or Talk Like a Pirate Day (or other "days"). For Women's History Month, I had images of my picture book biographies of women.

Entertains. When a story entertains, it brings plenty of WOM. This goes beyond just humor to create a story that sweeps up the audience into a story that is bigger-than-life, and leaves them engaged and happy.

Teaches. On the other hand, some stories are meant to teach. When they do this well, WOM is easy. The reader comes to this book/story with a problem, and the story teaches them the skills they need. Oh yes! They'll talk about this one.

Sharable. My daughter regularly bakes sugar cookies to sell. These are highly decorated works of art that taste amazing. When she posts on Facebook that a bunch of cookies are ready, she asks me to Share the post. But—often, she forgets to mark the post as Sharable. When you post on social media, always double check that the material is Sharable!

Luck. No doubt about it, it's hard to understand why this or that thing goes viral. There's always a sense of luck to WOM. You can do everything right—and bomb. Still. Do everything right. Sometimes, Lady Luck smiles on you.

Seed the Market

Give away as many books as you can. If one person has your book, they could shout from the roof and you'll never sell books. In fact, you need lots of someones to read your book and talk about it. One reason I submit to book awards is because it's my way of seeding the market. The people on the book award committees are influential in their respective areas. Even if a book doesn't win an award, the social studies teacher on the award committee might find that the book works perfectly for a class, or a summer camp, or just as a gift to their neighbor. A big chunk of my publicity budget goes to books for awards.

But I also try to give away using NetGalley (review service open to the public), Edelweiss (review service more geared to publishing industry), or Bookfunnel (give away ebooks through your website). You may even want to develop a formal street team or ARC (Advanced Reader Copy) team. Other review services open to indie books include Story Origin, Booksprout, Book Tasters, Book Sirens, or Hidden Gems. Check the sites to see if they have success with books similar to yours. Be on the lookout for other similar services that would benefit your books.

In the end, I try to keep a list of reviewers who will consistently look at my books with favor. They come from many sources, and I value them because they will help jumpstart that important WOM.

When I send out books, I often stuff the book with promotional material. For example, right now, I'm including a promo sheet about the illustrator. He has a robust schedule of library visits this summer, where he could sell books. I add any tidbits of information that will feed the WOM machine.

Grassroots

When I talk about grassroots marketing, I mean looking for places where you can develop a one-to-one relationship, usually with someone actually working with kids (since that's our audience). I know that certain reviewers, teachers, and parents will be interested in my next book. For those people, I try to give them something solid to talk about! Besides the book, they want and need the behind-the-scenes info. Develop that list of people who will consistently love your work and talk about it to others. See more in the Grassroots Marketing chapter.

Give them something to talk about!

Here are some things that people might talk about: cover reveal, great reviews, launch, milestones, and awards. Or perhaps, they want to know the story's inspiration, the trials and tribulations writing and publishing it, and where you received encouragement. Failures are great for WOM. Successes work, too.

Give them the right words

One important thing to remember is that you are giving your readers words with which to discuss your book. One reviewer of *Be Strong: The Rise of Beloved Public Art Sculptor Nancy Schön* told me that it would be a great book to read alongside of *Make Way for Ducklings*.

Yes, it's the story of the sculptor who took Robert McCloskey's two-dimensional drawings and created three-dimensional sculptures that live in Boston's Public Garden. Read it alongside McCloskey's book.

But it's far more than that.

When kids are frustrated by art, building, creating, athletics, or life, and they want to quit, sculptor Nancy Schön's story will inspire them with two simple words: Be Strong.

It's an inspirational story meant for kids who face creative problems and despair of ever finishing. It should be in every Makerspace area of every library. Lego moms and dads should read this to their kids to encourage creativity and perseverance with the lego building bricks. It's a social-emotional story of perseverance. Yes, Nancy Schön's story began with a duck family, but her story is bigger than that!

I try to put these words and ideas into the minds of everyone who reads this book! I'm seeding the discovery in the marketplace by giving away books; but I'm also seeding the conversation with statements about the book's place in children's literature. I want the WOM to take the book to new places!

$$\bullet \ \bullet \ \bullet \ \bullet \ \bullet \ \bullet \ \bullet$$

ACTION: For your next book's publicity and marketing tasks, answer this question: How does this add to the Word-of-Mouth conversation about this book?

Chapter 34
Newsletters or Email List

Newsletters start with the pre-publication phase but continue throughout the sales and marketing process. This involves collecting a reader's contact information, usually an email, and then emailing them news, information, updates, photos, videos, and other promotional material. When done well, a growing newsletter can generate sales. You'll find tons of information online on how to set up and run an email newsletter.

For children's books, the problem is we have a dual audience of adults and children. Safety laws for interacting with children online means that you should only target the adults, who are, after all, the ones who usually buy. Generally, this means you'll focus on parents or educators because each audience has special interests. Newsletters for educators will concentrate on integrating a book into their curriculum needs. Parents will focus more on entertaining a child. Obviously, there's an overlap between parent and educator needs, but it helps to know which you'll focus on.

Resources

The ins and outs of email newsletters is beyond the scope of this book. Look for books specifically written for authors or publishers, such as these:

Labrecque, Tammi. *Newsletter Ninja: How to Become an Author Mailing List Expert.* Larks and Katydids, c. 2018

Gaughran, David. *Strangers to Superfans: A Marketing Guide to the Reader Journey.* David Gaughran. c. 2020

• • • • • • •

ACTION: Decide if your newsletter will focus on parents or educators. Investigate mailing list providers and decide on which one you'll use for your newsletter.

Chapter 35
Advertising

E veryone Wants Your Money!
       But they can't have it unless...
       ...you get a penny back.

Here's the basic idea. Someone has an audience. You have a product meant for that audience. They say, give me $20 and in return, you'll make (at least) $20.01 in sales.

Advertising: The Exchange

Would you make that exchange? You get $0.01 profit for every $20 you spend? Yes. That is a positive Return on Investment (ROI). It's the basic premise of advertising that a message on the XXX platform will give you at least one penny ROI.

In our example of spending $20 for one cent ROI, that's only a .05% ROI, not so great. What if you got a 2% ROI, or $0.40? Much better. Let's say you spend $500, which earns you a 1% ROI of $505. $5 profit. Not bad. Of course, we'd prefer a 10% ROI, so that you'd earn $50 on that $500 investment.

Advertising works. You can sell your children's books with advertising and it can increase your overall profit. But you should understand the different types of advertising and popular platforms.

Some authors feel like advertising is "slimy," and they avoid it. The whole process of selling and advertising, in particular, feels beneath them as artists. It's just not right, they think. But I approach indie publishing as a small business. I work hard to produce a quality book that kids will love. And my business is to put a great book in the hands of the right kid. If I'm limited to only people I know, I'll sell few books. For marketing, you can do content marketing (such as blogs), social media (such as FB, Instagram, Blue Sky), newsletter marketing (i.e., gathering names, sending regular emails), school visits (i.e., speaking in person), and so on.

But what if you still don't reach your sales goals? Advertising is a way to increase sales on certain platforms, or in general, find a new audience. Remember, advertisers are selling you access to their audience. And in return...

Goal of Advertising

...you should get a sale or preorder. The goal of advertising—always for indies—is a sale. Never brand awareness and never traffic. Sales. Show me the money.

When you talk to experts from a platform, they often push you toward doing an awareness campaign. Run this ad for ten days, they say, to raise awareness of your brand, and then run a sales campaign.

If you set up an awareness campaign, what do you get from it? Someone has seen your book cover, and a few of those may have read your description from your ad. What good does that do you? Is that worth paying for? The experts say that it turns a cold audience (someone who knows nothing about you and your books) to a warm audience (someone who has some experience or knowledge of you and your books). Warm audiences are more likely to respond to advertising with a sale.

Yes, warm audiences respond better. But do you have enough extra cash to spend to warm up an audience? Usually not. I never run an ad just to warm up an audience. Your goals should always be for sales. Often an ad starts with some sales and you must tweak it (optimize it) to get a positive ROI or a better ROI. At least it started with sales. At least it has possibilities of a better ROI.

Cautions About Advertising

Before we start looking at more details, some caveats:

Do not spend money you don't have. Never borrow money to create ads.

Always remember that for any platform, you must learn their specific rules and nuances, and that means an investment of time. How much is your time worth? Factor that in somehow.

Your results may vary because each book is a unique combination of story, cover art, description, timing, your reputation, and so on. The only way to know if a platform will work for your book is to test.

I hate testing because it feels like a waste of money. But you must test platforms, audiences, images, and individual ads. On any given platform, one ad may do great and another may bomb. When you think about an advertising budget, allow something for testing. Still—overall—there should be a positive ROI.

Display Advertising

Display advertising is when you place an ad in a magazine or newspaper. This is more old school, but I still see people doing this. Targeted magazines, such as *Story Monsters*, are focused on those interested in children's literature. The audience is right! Is the price right? For this type media, you'll usually see a rate card that specifies the prices for various sizes of the ad and options for placement. The cover, for example, would be prime real estate and cost more. The problem?

How do you match up ads and sales? Is there a way to attribute this sale to that ad?

The problem of attribution is the most frustrating thing about display ads. It means it's very hard, if not impossible, to measure ROI. It may be possible if you send people to a dedicated page on your website. That is, sales from this page could only come from people who found it through that ad. Sometimes, you can use UTM tracking, which is a digital way to track clicks. It's beyond the scope of this book, but if you run ads that need to be tracked, search for more information on this technique. In general, it's hard to judge the ROI of display ads. For that reason, I seldom use this type of ad.

Distributor Catalogs

In the children's book world, many school districts or libraries use an educational distributor. These are companies who provide extra services to the school or library market to capture the sales. For example, if a school district wanted to use a book in a reading program and needed 500 copies, they could order from Amazon. But that would be a full-price retail purchase. Instead, an educational distributor can provide a hefty discount (10-25% or more), AND provide the information needed to catalog the book in the school library's data system. Many libraries or school districts work exclusively through an education or library distributor.

Which means, that distributor has the right audience for us. Their audience is customers (people actually buying children's books) who use the distributor's system to research and purchase books. And those distributors will offer you access to their audience with advertising.

Catalog advertising is the most common example of what the educational distributors offer. You can choose the size of the ad, and often add an author interview (for extra fee). They also offer advertising on their website, usually a banner ad (long, horizontal, usually at the top of a page, crossing all the columns). They are happy to send their rate cards or put you on their mailing list for notification of advertising availability. Often, they have targeted catalogs. For example, they might target STEM books, K-3 books, middle grade books, or series books as the focus for a certain catalog. Ads usually start at $250 or so, and can go up quickly, depending on add-ons.

I wish I could recommend these catalogs. After all, the audience is proven customers of children's books. But I've never had any luck with these. If it sounds interesting, check out Follett (Follett.com) for schools and Brodart (brodart.com/books) for library distribution.

CPC Ads

Most indie publishers prefer Cost Per Click (CPC) ads over display ads. These are online ads, which means the platforms have the capability to track each click and provide mostly accurate attribution: this click resulted in that sale. It allows you to measure with some confidence the ROI of your advertising. And that's very important. (Of course, some will argue about the accuracy of a certain system's tracking, but that's another story.)

The main CPC platforms for children's books include Facebook/Meta ads, Amazon ads, and Bookbub ads. IngramID ads will aggregate this for you and place ads on the appropriate platform.

Each advertising platform has quirks related to their own technology. But we can still generalize about how this works.

1. **Hooks.** You create text and images that should hook your reader and get them interested in your book.
2. **Audience.** Next, you decide on the audience. Each platform lets you choose audiences, but the methods differ.
   a. Bookbub lets you target readers of other books, but these must be readers active on the Bookbub platform. You must research an author's popularity on Bookbub to determine if they have enough readers

to be worth targeting. After choosing comparable authors, you can also add a category. This is helpful because some authors have popular books in several genres. For example, James Patterson has audiences of readers of thrillers and children's books. If you target him, you'll also want to add the category of children's books.

b. Amazon ads lets you target by keywords (topics, author names), ASIN (specific products), or categories. In addition, you can decide if you want exact matches, near matches, or broad matches. It means testing your approach to audience for your particular book.

c. Facebook/Meta has started relying more heavily on artificial intelligence for targeting ads. They are starting to prefer that you leave the audience to them, confident that their AI can match an ad to an audience. The results are mixed so far; as usual, romance and thriller authors tend to have better results. It means, a longer and more expensive testing phase before you see results. Unfortunately, FB/Meta are moving toward making the A.I. audiences mandatory. As of this writing, you can still add keywords such as "children's literature," narrow by demographic categories such as "parents of 9-12 yo," limit age ranges, and limit to a certain country. But the options are narrowing as FB/Meta invests in its A.I. technology.

3. **Bids and Budgets.** Amazon lets you monitor how much each click costs, and you can raise/lower bids for each keyword. A bid means that you think a click is worth XX amount and will pay up to that amount. To figure this, you also need to know how many clicks you get before a sale results. If you get one click for every ten

impressions (or the # times the ad is shown), that's a reasonable 10% Buy Through Rate. If you only get one sale per hundred clicks, it's hard to make a profit on books, which are relatively low profit margins. Again - you must test and track your ads. You can also set a budget, or a daily spend limit, on your ads. Bookbub also lets you bid on clicks, but there are two options. You can pay for impressions or clicks. Paying by impressions means that they will charge the fee you set for views. For example, it may be $12.00 for 1000 views. You hope that you'll have enough click through (monitor the CTR or Click Through Rate), that you make sales and turn a profit. This can rapidly give you an idea of how effective an audience target may be. But most people prefer to set a price per click; you only pay if someone clicks on your ad. On the other hand, Facebook/Meta focuses on setting a budget for the campaign, rather than bids per click. If you decide to spend $100/day, Meta will try to spend that. Again, experiences vary widely and you should study the platform before jumping in.

Regardless of which platform you choose, it's wise to study the platform's quirks. I suggest reading several books for each platform because many books are explaining how that author earned on the ad platform. Rarely, though, are they children's book authors. What applies to Romantasy YA titles, will likely not apply to children's literature.

Resources

Here are some books about advertising that I've read and respect. Always look for the most up-to-date information since the platforms change constantly. Like—constantly! Still, the older books give you great basic information on the platforms and ways to think about ads.

The thought processes are as important as anything as you look at these platforms. And look for information on selling books via ads, as there are nuances.

- Fayet, Ricardo. Amazon Ads for Authors: Unlock Your Full Advertising Potential (2023)
- Gaughran, David. Bookbub Ads Expert (2019)
- Potter, Deb. Amazon Ads for Authors (2019)

Author and self-publishing guru, David Gaughran also has a newsletter chock full of info about advertising—highly recommended. Sign up here: https://davidgaughran.com/following-free-newsletter/

CPC advertising is a Wild West environment with constant change and turmoil. Gurus show up regularly touting a certain approach to advertising on a certain platform. First, be skeptical that their approach is the best one for children's books; we are the odd man out in most business decisions like this.

Second, read as much free material on the author, their approach, their successes, and their failures as you can. Look for podcasts, blog posts, and Facebook groups. Before you spend money on an expensive course, do your research. The course may or may not give you that all-important ROI.

This has been a quick overview of advertising for children's books. I think there's a place for ads in the overall mix of marketing activities. For some titles, and for some time periods, advertising can boost your income. Whatever you decide, don't let anyone take your hard-earned money, unless they give you at least a penny profit!

• • • • • • •

ACTION: Choose one advertising platform to study. If you publish with KDP, the Amazon advertising is a logical choice. Plan to study or take courses on how to advertise on this platform. Start slowly and monitor your ROI! After you master one program, you can add others.

Chapter 36
Reviews

The next pre-publication task to tackle is reviews. Reviews work as social proof to prospective readers by reassuring them that others enjoyed your book. You need a minimum of ten reviews, but hundreds of reviews is much better! For legacy published authors, some of this is done by the publisher, but often authors are encouraged to reach out to their contacts and offer a review copy. As indie publishers, we can offer print or digital ARCs (Advance Reader Copy) as review copies.

For Digital ARCs

Netgalley is an online platform that allows a publisher/author to upload a book and offer a digital download. There are fees for this, which can be several hundred dollars, so look for organizations that offer a discount or easy ways to participate. NetGalley is used by librarians, journalists, avid readers, and more.

Edelweiss is the alternative service, also paid, for digital review copies, but they seem to focus more on the industry of journalists, bookstore buyers, library staff, and award committee members.

I like to say that NetGalley is outward focused on the public, but Edelweiss is inward focused on the industry.

Finally, Bookfunnel is widely used by indie publishers to distribute ebooks and audiobooks. When you make a sale on your website store, the ebook and audiobook are sent over immediately from Bookfunnel. They also provide several strategies for sending books out for review. The service charges a yearly fee.

Or, you can simply offer a low-resolution pdf for review. This works well in many cases.

Consider sending copies to influential local, state, and regional people. Look for officers of local literacy organizations, reading councils, state librarians, and so on. To submit to awards, you must also send copies of the book. Often the timetable for the award requires they be sent before the book is published. Books published in August to November may be sent to award committees in this pre-publication phase.

Review Journals

For children's books, there are a limited number of review journals. You must send these at least three months before publication, and some have moved to a four-month lead time. For each of these review journals, research at their current requirements for submissions.

- *Kirkus*. This is a paid review, so look for discounts. Visit their website, then look for a discount offer as they remarket to you on Facebook or other social media platforms.
- *School Library Journal*
- *Booklist Online*
- *Bulletin for the Center of Children's Books*
- *Foreword Reviews*

Also, look for specialized review sources pertinent to your book.

For example, Locus magazine reviews science fiction and fantasy books.

• • • • • • •

ACTION: Decide on a strategy for sending out ARCs

Decide on which review journals are appropriate for your book and study their submission guidelines before submitting.

Chapter 37
Marketing to Educators

I f you distribute through educational distributors, be sure to send review copies or sell sheets about 3 months early. This means you must plan your publication schedule to allow you to print copies early for this marketing effort. This includes places such as Follett School Solutions, Mackin, Children's Plus, Permabound, and so on.

Some of these companies have a curriculum department which will evaluate your book to see how it fits into curriculums across the U.S. For each state, they will create suggested reading lists for subject areas, such as second grade science books. You want your book listed on as many of those suggested lists as possible. Unfortunately, there's not much you can do about this except to understand the curriculum needs and plan for them as closely as possible.

Reading Programs

Accelerated Reader is a reading program popular in some schools. They provide quizzes for books so the teacher can evaluate a child's comprehension skills.

If your book receives a starred review or other awards, submit to Accelerated Reader and ask them to create a quiz for your book.

Send review copies to Title Selection Coordinator, Renaissance Learning, Inc., 2911 Peach Street, Wisconsin Rapids, WI 54494.

For other reading programs, get Lexile Levels, a measurement of the difficulty of the text, on each title. See the Metadata chapter for more information. Include this information in all communications and on your website.

Guides to Your Book

Educators appreciate when a book has a Teacher's Guide, which includes curriculum-related material. You may specialize this as a Discussion Guide or a Book Club Guide. As you create guides, remember that these should tie into the curriculum. For science, that's the NextGen Science Standards. Other teacher groups have similar curriculum standards, available by searching. Don't forget that the school counselors have Social Emotional Learning (SEL) standards.

The guides vary widely from 4 to 40 pages, and there's no standard. Instead, work to make sure you are meeting the needs of a busy teacher. I always keep in mind that a teacher's motto is "Make My Life Easy." Give them activity sheets to photocopy, questions tailored to the curriculum, and innovative ideas. They should be able to pick it up and be live in their classroom within minutes. For more see Teacher's Guides with AI (https://www.indiekidsbooks.com/p/teach ers-guides-with-ai)

Teachers Pay Teachers (TPT)

TPT is a website that caters to teachers by providing lesson plans, including worksheets to photocopy. As implied by the name, most vendors are teachers. But anyone can add lessons to the site and sell them. If you have a strong background in education, you may want to sell your guides or activities on TPT.

YouTube Channel

Finally, consider a YouTube channel. Our audience, the Alpha Generation, is online and YouTube is especially favored up to 10 years old. Create a fun channel that includes a variety of activities. Consider reading aloud, adding audiobooks, behind-the-scenes information, interviews, and more. It's a big commitment to creating a YouTube channel, but this is one place your audience likes to hang out.

• • • • • • •

ACTION: If teachers and educators are your market, decide how to approach this market segment. Will you contact educational distributors, obtain Lexile reading levels, or create teacher's guides?

Study TPT and YouTube as possible ways to reach the audience. Are either of these appropriate for your books?

Chapter 38
KU or Wide?

K DP Select is a free 90-day promotional program for Kindle eBooks only. After enrolling in KDP Select, you have the opportunity to reach more readers through Amazon and Kindle promotions. All authors, regardless of where they live, are eligible. It requires an exclusive listing, which means you cannot sell your ebook anywhere else while the book is in this program. If you are also distributed by educational distributors, reading apps, or plan a Kickstarter, then you can't use KU. When you add your book to KDP Select, it is automatically enrolled in Kindle Unlimited, or KU.

KU is a subscription service for readers who have paid a fee for unlimited access to books in the program. It's popular with certain genres, such as romance and science fiction.

The advantage of KDP Select is that your book is offered free to those in the Kindle Unlimited (KU) and Kindle Owners' Lending Library (KOLL) program, an estimated 2.5 million readers who typically read 5 books/month. This is often a great thing for children's books. You're paid by "KENP," or Kindle Edition Normalized Page reads. It's been running less than $0.005/page. It takes a lot of reads

231

for children's books to earn much. Still, kids do read on apps, and it's one app that is available to even beginning publishers. Bonuses are possible, but children's books are included in the general category for bonuses, so they are harder to achieve. (See more on the bonuses: https://kdp.amazon.com/en_US/help/topic/G201623400)

When you sign up for KU, it's a 90-day commitment, and you can opt out after that with no problem. It's just clicking a button. This makes KDP Select/KU an easy thing to try for your books. Some people try KU for the first 90 days after publication and then opt out to try other strategies.

In the self-publishing world, "Going Wide" means that you do NOT sign up for KDP Select/KU, which means you have NOT agreed to be exclusive on Amazon.

How to Choose Between Wide and KU

Check your book's category on Amazon, and then check out the best-sellers in that category. How many of them are in Kindle Unlimited, that is, are offered free to subscribers? If your category is full of KU books, consider trying the program. If few books in your category are in KU, it's likely not popular with your readers.

Remember that KU isn't forever. You agree to a 90-day commitment, and after that you can easily opt out. It makes for easy testing to see if your book will gain traction on that platform.

If you're enrolled in KDP Select, check out the promotions that they offer as part of the program. You can set up Free Days or Count-down Days. Use these wisely to market the book, focusing on downloads. For full and current information, see this support page: https://kdp.amazon.com/en_US/help/topic/G200798990

As a business practice, I don't like putting all my trust in one company. If you put all your books in KU, then you're at the mercy of Amazon's whims. However, for the right books, you may make more money in the short run by going all in with KU. It's an individual decision and can vary from book to book.

Get David Gaughran's free ebook, *Amazon Decoded* https://davidgaughran.com/

Then read this blog post: A Tale of Two Marketing Systems by David Gaughran. https://davidgaughran.com/2017/10/23/a-tale-of-two-marketing-systems/

Marketing Wide

If you choose not to participate in KDP Select/KU, then you'll want to offer your books for sale on as many platforms as possible. It takes time to build an audience on other platforms, often 3-12 months before the income level increases. It also means that you must learn the ins and outs of each platform. GooglePlay is quite different from Apple's iTunes!

I look for and add other distributors whenever possible. See the Distributions chapter.

Resources

Monica Leonelle writes a series of books, *Book Sales Supercharged*, which explain sales on specific platforms. Look for the specific books for platforms you wish to try. As always, you'll have to translate strategies to children's books, but these books give you a place to start.

• • • • • • •

ACTION: Decide on your strategy regarding Kindle Unlimited. Will you enroll your book for the first 90-days or will you stay enrolled indefinitely? Or will you choose to go wide right away?

Chapter 39
Catalogs

O ne marketing tool that helps me sell books is a catalog of Mims House books. My publishing company, Mims-HouseBooks (https://mimshousebooks.com/pages/catalog) now has a nice backlist. But even if you only have a couple of books, I'd urge you to create your own catalog because they are so useful for marketing.

Note: I don't print multiple copies to mail out. Instead, I print these when needed. I have two versions, one which is high quality for printing, and one lower quality with a smaller file size that makes it perfect for e-mailing or downloading from the website. If I ever need it, I can print high-quality glossy catalogs at a local printer.

Where to Use a Catalog

Let's look at places to use a catalog.

Conferences. I often print the entire catalog and distribute at conferences. I may be speaking about one particular book, but I want the audience to know that I've got a range of books. Particularly helpful is the ordering form included at the back of the catalog. Librarians and teachers grab them up.

Educational distributors. My books are distributed through educational distributors. It's essential to let those partners know what books are coming out. Sending them seasonal catalogs is an easy way to update them.

Also, I often get requests for a price quote from educational distributors. A local teacher, school, or school district wants a price on X copies of Y title. The catalog streamlines the process, making it easy to give them the information they need.

Foreign Rights. Another request I often get is for information on foreign rights. For each book listed in the catalog, I note what rights have been sold, so international publishers will see what's available. This has been important in getting a 9-book deal from a Chinese publisher and a 6-book deal from a Korean publisher.

Website links. On the Catalog Page of my website, I offer the full catalog, which includes the ordering form, as downloads. They are a popular download.

For myself. The catalog is also useful for myself! When I need a quick memory jog of the pricing of a particular book, I pull out the catalog. I don't link to the old catalogs online, but for myself, it's also a milestone every year to compare the previous year's catalogs and see progress.

Creating a Catalog

So, how do you create a catalog? First, you can scope out catalogs from your favorite publishers and get ideas to copy. Look at the type of copy they use, what metadata information is included, special offers, and so on. When you have ideas of how you want to approach it, then you're faced with layout and design.

I make it simple for myself by going over to GraphicRiver.net and search for catalog or brochure templates. For under $20, you can usually find a great-looking template that fits your needs. You need an imagination to see your books in the catalog instead of fashion, but I find the templates to be a good starting point, especially since the page numbers, headers and footers are already worked out.

Or, if you're a Canva.com fan, use their templates.

Just like your books, be sure to proofread your catalog.

I prefer to update my catalog twice a year with new titles. Look at your publishing program to see if you need yearly updates or updates on some other schedule.

• • • • • • •

ACTION: Create a simple catalog for your publishing program. Offer it as a download on your website, or hand it out at a conference. Based on feedback, decide if this is an effective marketing asset for your books.

Chapter 40
Preorders and Crowd Funding

F inally, one strategy is to include preorders in your marketing mix. This means setting up books early on Amazon, the publisher's website, ebook platforms such as Apple or GooglePlay, or other online platforms. Once the book is set up, you can start to market it, just as you will once the book launches. For legacy publishers, strong preorders can indicate a book that may break out. For indie publishers, it means that something is working well, and the book may have a long and prosperous life.

A second way to collect preorders is to use a Kickstarter campaign. In the early days of Kickstarter, many considered it a method to bring in capital to fund things such as print runs. Today, many indie publishers use it as a preorder campaign.

The Kickstarter audience is different from the Amazon audience, and you have the advantage of collecting customer contact information that can be added to your newsletter. I started paying attention when one well-known author said that Kickstarter was his favorite social media platform. I hadn't thought of it as a social media platform! If you treat it like one, though, you can join the community by supporting other campaigns, read and learn from other campaigns, and build a following so that each of your book campaigns builds on the previous ones.

Campaigns with small goals from $500-1000 are a common way to slowly build that audience. Kickstarter buyers are often your super-fans, the ones who love your work and want you to succeed. They become an audience who spreads your work through word of mouth. Kickstarter campaigns require careful setup and marketing, and lots of effort, but can pay off as a long-term strategy.

If you decide to do a crowd-funding program as a preorder, plan ahead. Crowd-funding platforms take time and care to set up correctly, and reward books are typically sent 1-6 months after the campaign ends. You won't want to publish the book on major platforms until your Kickstarter supporters receive their books. A Kickstarter can add 3-12 months to the publication timeline.

Resources

Sharp, Anthea L. *Kickstarter for Authors: Empowering Writers to Fund and Flourish.* Fiddlehead Press, c. 2023.

· · · · · · ·

ACTION: For your preferred platforms, study the process for setting up preorders and try it for your next book. Evaluate if it's an effective strategy for your books.

Study Kickstarter as a possible marketing program. Start by reading Anthea Sharp's book, and studying current Kickstarter projects. Decide if it's a strategy you want to try for your books.

Part Six
Marketing during Launch

Launch

It's time! Your book is about to launch into the world. You'll need all the marketing strategies discussed in the pre-publication phase, but there are some special tasks for the launch phase. Mostly, you'll be launching special events designed to highlight the book and earn those crucial early sales. Gaining momentum on all platforms will help raise the book's profile. On Amazon, especially, if you can pull off great sales in the first month of sales, the algorithms will reward you with even higher visibility.

Chapter 41
Launch

Launching your book is about creating a lot of excitement in a short amount of time. The launch period can last one day or as long as six months, but it's hard to maintain excitement over the longer time periods. Usually, the excitement comes from social media strategies, interviews, advertising, and special events. The goal is to move a lot of books in a short amount of time. If you manage this, then your Amazon rankings go up and it's more likely that Amazon's algorithm will kick in to recommend your book. The book's perceived popularity becomes a self-fulfilling loop which results in more sales.

First, use all the strategies from the pre-publication phase. Double check all metadata. Give readers a reason to remember your name and use talking points for word-of-mouth discussions. Send messages to your newsletter or mailing list folks. Advertise the book on appropriate platforms.

Social Media Strategies

Social media allows us to create content and publish it to reach the right audience. The options today are so wide and diverse that I can't explain specifics of any particular platform. You can choose video for TikTok or Instagram. Or choose a series of images on Facebook and BlueSky. Or you could create a dedicated YouTube channel for your books.

To post on social media, you will use text, images, audio, or video. I suggest authors look at their strongest medium, the one they can consistently create, and choose a social media platform that supports that. If you love short-form video, try YouTube, TikTok, or Instagram. However, if you like long-form video, focus on YouTube. If you like short-form text, try X, BlueSky, or Threads. If you prefer long-form text, try Substack, WordPress, or Beehive.

Whatever medium you choose, your goal is to consistently post and build an audience on that platform. The strategies you choose will strengthen your platform and show off your personality and books in a unique way.

Don't try to do all the platforms! Choose a home base and a couple satellite platforms and focus.

Interviews & Publicity

Blogs, podcasts, legacy newspapers or magazines—there are many options for interviews. One publicity specialist suggested that you write a list of 50 or 100 things that you could write or talk about with some expertise. Then look for publications devoted to a niche that you can intelligently discuss something. Repeat for each of the 50 things you can expertly discuss! The interviews don't have to be about the specific book; you're just looking for coverage for you as the expert, and in your bio, you'll list the book.

In other words, there are many places to get the word out about your book through an interview. The key is to focus on the intersection of your book, your audience, and your expertise in an area. When those converge, it's a good place to be interviewed.

Time interviews for a month before to a month after the launch. The goal is to build anticipation for the book and your author career, and to generate sales.

Local and Regional Events

Craft fairs, PTA events, library story time—local and regional events can vary widely, and you'll have to judge where to spend your time and energy. Look for low overhead, the right audience, and your enthusiasm for the event. Keep in mind your profit margins to calculate whether you'll make money or lose money. For example, my local zoo does Boo at the Zoo for Halloween, but to rent a table costs $500, too much for my budget. I would need to sell 100 books or more to earn back the fees, so it's not an event for me. However, a book-signing at a local library should be profitable and fun.

Look around at events to which you can easily drive in half a day, so you don't have to spend the night and pay for a hotel. If I can get to an event, participate, and then drive home that night, I'm more likely to participate. I look for literacy fairs, conferences for teachers, librarians, or parents, and regional arts and craft events.

Newsletters, Discount or Free

There are several newsletters which advertise free or discounted books. One launch strategy is to plan a price promotion and stack newsletters around that promotion. For example, you may discount an eBook to free for the first three days. You might book a promo with three or four newsletters to maximize the impact.

It might seem counterintuitive to discount to free during the book's first week. That's when you logically want to earn back your investment. But some would argue that the real goal is to gain visibility, so the book has a chance of long-term success. This strategy means you forgo early income in return for seeding the marketplace with books, and hope the readers love it enough to talk about it to their friends. Remember—word of mouth sells books!

Newsletters that include promotions for children's books are limited, and the landscape changes frequently. When a reader signs up for the newsletter, they can usually indicate the genres that interest them. The newsletter should tell you how many subscribers are in each category, including children's books or teen books. Remember that when you send out a newsletter—even promotional newsletters like this—30% open rate is considered good. So, if the newsletter says they have an audience of 10,000 readers looking for free children's books, they will consider it acceptable if 3,000 opened the email. A click-through rate of 30% is optimistic. That would give you 900 people who click through to see your book. And there, if you get a 5% purchase rate, you may have 45 sales/giveaways, for an optimistic guess. The diminishing return for each step means it's crucial to see the subscriber rates. It re-emphasizes the importance of the book cover and title!

When you're ready to launch, search current availability for newsletters that include children's categories. Meanwhile, these are some of the classic sites:

- Bookbub.com
- Fussy Librarian
- BookDoggy
- BookRaid
- Freebooksy

• • • • • • •

ACTION: Several months before your next launch, take the time to create a detailed launch plan. Consider social media strategies, interviews and publicity, local and regional events, and using newsletters. Take the time to write out and consider all the options. Then, execute the plan! Based on feedback, revise for the next launch.

Chapter 42
School Visits

When you read about indie publishing of children's books, inevitably the marketing discussion turns to school visits. Planning school visits close to your launch makes sense because sales at the school can bring added income in this crucial phase. Of course, you'll continue school visits for as long as you pursue your career.

Yo-Yos or Books?

Many years ago, when I was just starting out with one book published, I went to a school to talk about my book. The week before, the school had invited the YoYo People to come and entertain. They were paid $1000, and they were allowed to send home flyers to sell yo-yos.

For my visit, I was paid nothing, was barely acknowledged by the school administration, and I had to buy my own lunch.

I vowed that I would never again do free visits (except for family or close friends). I am more educational than yo-yos. And I'm even entertaining. I deserve compensation.

So, why does everyone assume that we should do school visits? There are two great reasons to do school visits—and one big caution. Let's look at them, and then I'll give you resources for planning and executing your visits.

Know Your Audience

The first reason has nothing to do with marketing. Instead, I'd urge you to visit schools to learn more about your audience. You'll talk to kids, teachers, and librarians. I always try to informally ask kids what they are reading these days. It's interesting to hear the popular books and the books that are never mentioned. You get a sense of the popular culture within the elementary community right now.

You also get a sense of the vocabulary level, interests, dislikes, and so much more of the kids themselves. Don't just "do a school visit." Go with curiosity and a desire to know what would make these kids laugh, cry, dig in, or reject a story.

When you do the presentation, pay attention to when the kids are listening, hanging onto every word. Or when they are restless, turning to chat with friends, bored. The presentations will give you real-life, real-time feedback on your story.

Also, pay attention to teachers and librarians. Where do they buy books? Ask them! What is their favorite book this year? Favorite author? Do they read aloud to the kids? How many books does each class check out weekly?

In other words, school visits are an opportunity to do in-depth market research! Go with curiosity and take notes!

Fast, Easy Income

A second reason to do school visits is to generate fast, easy income. Speaking fees range from $100–$3000, with the top fees earned by the winner of the Newbery Award, the top children's award from the

American Library Association. That means locally, you'll likely be in the range of $300–1000.

Variables can include how many presentations, how long, whether they will allow you to sell books, travel distance and arrangements, and other details.

For example, for presentations within my small state of Arkansas, I might ask for $650 for up to four presentations that day. That could be large group, small group, talking to parents at a PTA meeting, or a staff development presentation, their choice. But no more than four.

In other words, be sure to discuss the details of the visit. I usually also ask for a gluten-free meal for lunch, a microphone and PowerPoint projection system, and travel reimbursement. Schools are used to using the federal government's rate for travel reimbursement, and this is almost always part of the fees, no argument.

Book Sales During a School Visit

In addition, you should ask to sell books. Always prepare an order form to send home with students. Some people prefer to send these a week early and let kids bring them back to school on the day of the presentation. That way, you bring books that day to sign and sell.

Some, however, prefer to present and then send home an order form that's due the next week. Some report better sales because the kids have already seen and heard them. But it means another trip to deliver the books or a shipping fee.

Either way is fine, but you should sell books somehow! It's fine to add "bundle pricing," such as "Buy All 3 Books for 25% discount."

How many books will you sell? It depends. (Doesn't everything "depend"?) In a wealthy area, you might sell to 30–50% of a school's population. For a school with 300 kids, that's 90–150 books. In a poor area, you may sell 2–3% of the school's population. For a school with 300 kids, that's 6–9 books.

In general, though, I plan on selling to 5–10% of a school's population. For that 300-kid school, I would take 30 books with me and plan to ship the rest. Your results will vary, but after a couple visits, you should be able to guess at sales.

Build Your Reputation

A final reason to do school visits is to build your reputation and name recognition.

As we discussed earlier, Peter Hildick-Smith says, "It's hard to form a loyalty to an author if you don't even know their name." Some authors spend the first couple years of their career visiting schools for the purpose of building their name recognition and pumping up book sales.

It's definitely one option to build your career, but it has limits.

One Big Caution

It sounds like school visits are a wonderful opportunity! So, what's the big caution?

The problem is that you can't scale up income from school visits. There are only 180 or so days in a school year (depending on your country, state, etc.). Can you do 180 school visits per year? No! It's physically exhausting to continuously go and go and go.

Most authors try to schedule a week at a time so that they can plan their writing schedule. Or perhaps they plan a summer of library visits (similar to school visits, but a different venue). That schedule is even tighter for an indie publisher who has to do writing, contracts, layout and design, marketing, and everything else.

You cannot do 300 school visits a year. It's physically impossible.

That's why I consider school visits a strategy for early in a career. When you just have one or two books out, and you need that extra cash—go for it! You'll start to build your reputation, learn your audience, and put money in your pocket. It's a great gig.

But as your career develops, you should also be developing other ways of marketing and selling books, other income streams. You should start selling bulk to school districts, earn a steady income on KDP, develop your audience on OverDrive (library ebooks and audiobooks), and so much more.

In ten years, if you're still relying on school visits as your main income source—I'm sorry for you.

You must see school visits as an important income stream, yes. But you can't scale it up, like you can other income streams, because it requires you to be physically present, doing nothing else except concentrating on that performance. That means it's an important step in the development of your career, but one that you should plan to eventually outgrow.

UNLESS—and this is a big one!—I do know authors who are performers at heart. They live to be in front of the kids. When they write, they plan and dream about reading the book aloud to large groups. These performers excel at school visits, and they will likely never be happy without that performance aspect of their work. For them, school visits are crucial to their happiness. Great! I do hope they also develop other income streams, though, so they can be picky about which speaking invitations to accept.

Resources for School Visits

Planning and executing school visits can seem daunting, but like everything else in the indie publishing life, you can learn to do this.

First, be sure to get the details of a visit ironed out before you agree. That would be compensation, speaking location or venue, how many presentations, topics of presentations, clear understanding of audience, travel arrangements, and so on.

SchoolVisitExperts.com is a huge resource for you because they provide advice and help on all the nitty-gritty details. Run by Alexis O'Neill, it's packed with info. While you're at it, study Alexis's website, too, for details on how she does visits. For example, download her pdf of her School Visit Checklist, which is meant for school personnel. She also has sample schedules, signed bookmarks to print, book order form, and more. Her book, *The Recess Queen*, is one of my all-time favorite books.

Aren't we lucky? Our audience regularly gathers in local schools for 8 hours per day. We can easily reach out to teachers, librarians, or administrators and plan a day to visit them. During that visit, your curiosity will let you learn so much about your audience that you'll come back with new ideas, or tweaks to old ideas. You gain confidence that your work resonates with the kids. By the way, you add income—always a welcome outcome.

Plan now for ways to reach out and find more school visits for the next school year!

• • • • • • •

ACTION: Based on your book, decide on three programs you could offer to schools. It could be something about the book's topic, your writing process, or simply reading the book. Write a short paragraph about each school program.

Decide on your fees for a program and any other parameters necessary for your program (powerpoint, microphone, etc.)

Then, send your proposal to ten schools! Start local, but also consider schools that might have a special interest in your book's topic.

Chapter 43
Swag & Merch

The opportunities for swag (giveaway items) and merch (items to sell) are myriad: pens, pencils, cups, t-shirts, stickers, plush animals, related toys, computer mouse pads, blank books, puzzles, motivational bracelets, bookmarks, and so on. What makes sense for your book?

If you wrote a fantasy novel, you could give away a custom printed map of the world. For a picture book about horses, perhaps a stuffed horse would be perfect. A blank book with a beautiful cover might appeal to readers of a romance. Think about your audience and what merchandise will appeal to them.

Just as there are POD printers for books, there are POD printers for swag: Printify, Printful, and so on. Using a POD service limits your initial layout, but items will cost more. You'll have to decide if buying in bulk or using a POD service makes sense. The POD companies will integrate with multiple online sales platforms, so confirm that they will work with your preferred platforms.

Always try to calculate your ROI (return on investment, or how much profit you'll make) and use that to inform your decisions.

Swag can be used at launch parties, special sales, holidays, school visits, or at special events. I rarely do swag because I'm not a party girl! But it works for many authors.

• • • • • • •

ACTION: If swag and merch are exciting to you, figure out how to make it work. Investigate possible POD printers, local sources, and online sources for swag and merch related to your book. Create a budget and market. Start small and watch your budget! And have fun!

Part Seven
Marketing Post-Publication

After one to six months, your book officially passes to a post-publication status. After a year, it's generally considered to be backlist. In the traditional world, your book must find its audience quickly, or it will go out of print. But as an independent publisher, you can continue to market your book for the life of the copyright, your lifetime, plus seventy years.

You can and should employ any marketing strategies from pre-publication or launch periods that make sense. For example, building a strong email list will be a task for most of your career. But there are a few added marketing strategies for backlist titles. Let's look at what's possible.

Chapter 44
Metadata Updates

O
n April 8, 2024, a solar eclipse crossed a large swath of the U.S. For my book, *Eclipse*, I updated metadata to reference the event. By adding a single sentence to the opening of the description, I made the book timely and relevant.

In the pre-publication discussion of marketing, I spent a lot of time emphasizing metadata because it's a crucial part of the discovery phase. But it's also a crucial part of continuing to sell a book for a long time period.

Ideas for Regular Updates to Metadata

1. Update all information for special events such as the 2023 solar eclipse. Be sure to update after the event, too!
2. New book covers are a staple of the industry. If a book is selling poorly, a new cover might help revive it, especially if paired with a promotion or a lead up to a special event. If the book is a couple years old, you may consider a new cover to refresh it to appeal to today's readers. It's not

unusual for books to receive a new cover every five years or so.

3. Update your biography to highlight books from your growing bibliography. If you win awards or other special events occur, update those.

4. The BISAC codes update regularly, too. Be sure to use the up-to-date categories for BISAC, or for LOC/LCSH and Thema codes. You can change these at any point, so if books aren't selling well, consider looking for better categories.

Always work to keep your metadata consistent and up-to-date. This is one of the main ways that readers will continue to find your books.

• • • • • • •

ACTION: Create a schedule and calendar alerts reminders to do yearly metadata checks for all your books in print. At the same time, evaluate whether books need a new cover.

Chapter 45
Editions

Your book is out! It's set in stone, right? Wrong. You may need special or second editions of the book.

A special edition means that you've created a unique format that includes different formatting or somehow changes the book's physical appearance.

Second editions of a title means that you have substantially updated the book in some way, changing or adding over 10% of the text. This is more common in nonfiction books when information needs to be updated.

When do you need a special edition? A second edition?

Special Editions

Here are some reasons to create a special edition of your book! As you create special editions, work to build a community of readers and your author reputation. Remember, you want readers to know your name and be waiting for your next book. Offering a beautiful special edition makes you stand out from the crowd. If you make substantial changes, you'll need a new ISBN.

1. **Bookclub edition.** If your audience loves book clubs, you could add Book Club Discussion Questions to the book to create a special Book Club Edition, with a special cover. This one may need a separate ISBN because of the additional material for this audience.

2. **Kickstarter edition.** If you run a Kickstarter fundraising project, you could create a special edition of the book with sprayed edges, ribbons, or other premium features. Or, combine it with other books in a series to create a boxed set.

3. **Anniversary editions.** Is your book ten years old and still popular? Create a special anniversary edition to celebrate. Perhaps, add an author interview or other features to make it a collector's item (which might require a special ISBN). Or add the painted edges or other special printing details.

4. **Limited editions.** If your book has become popular with a certain demographic, you might coordinate with an organization to create a special edition. Or perhaps, a customer wants to use your book for a subscription service but needs some customization. When Little Passports decided to use my book, *Nefertiti, the Spidernaut*, in their subscription box service, they asked for a special edition. Instead of 8.5" x 8.5", we printed it 8" x 8", and co-branded it with Little Passports logo on the corner of the front cover. I only printed the quantity they ordered, so it was a limited special edition.

5. **White label editions.** White label means you have a book that is blank of branding, and you sell that to an organization or company who will add their own branding. For example, if you wrote a cookbook for kids, you could white label the book to a company that sells cookware. The cookware company would add their branding and sell (or give away) the book as if they had

created it. You would negotiate a fee based on the quantity needed, and the customizations agreed upon. This probably needs its own ISBN.

6. **Collector's edition.** When Brandon Sanderson ran his Kickstarter program that earned over $41 million, he created special collector's editions with faux-leather binding and special artwork. A collector's edition implies that the physical book is enhanced someway with premium materials: special paper, ribbon bookmarks, special binding material, embossing, gilded cover, map for the endpapers, extra artwork, etc. These are most often associated with Kickstarter campaigns, but you could do it at any time.

7. **Signed editions.** Or, create a special, limited edition that you have signed! One idea is to use books in stock that haven't sold, sign them and market as signed editions. Will that help sell your books? It depends on why you have leftover copies. If the book sells well in general, and it's odd to have these leftover books, this might work. If the book sells poorly, the sales potential is less, but it could still work if you have a targeted audience for this edition. How much is your signature worth? The only way to know is to test it.

Second Edition

A second edition means you have updated the material of the book by at least 10%, and you need readers to know that it is an updated version. This happens most often for nonfiction which updates when new information is added. But it can also happen for fiction if you revise heavily, add or subtract a new chapter and so on. Second editions do need new ISBNs, because they are a different book.

My book, *Novel Metamorphosis: Uncommon Ways to Revise* was

a second edition when I updated the information and added chapters. That meant a new ISBN.

When you created your book, you actually created intellectual property that can sell for years. Keep it fresh with new covers, new editions, and new ways to present it to your audience.

• • • • • • •

ACTION: Yearly, evaluate your books for possible special or second editions. Always be alert for possible ways to market via a special or second edition.

Chapter 46
Audience Connections

One of the most important tasks of the post-launch period is to find ways to connect with your audience. Depending on your book, you should have a good idea of who is most likely to purchase your books. Here are ideas for different market segments.

Educators. If educators are a strong audience for you, consider providing teacher's guides, discussion guides, or book club guides. Consider using Teachers Pay Teachers to sell those extra materials. Attend local, regional, or national educator conferences. Create Pinterest boards around appropriate topics. Or perhaps you enjoy video and could sustain a YouTube channel about your topics and ideas.

Parents. Parents love buying books for their kids! Find ways to connect through local or regional events, podcasts for parents, and being interviewed as an expert in literacy in the media.

Bookstores. For local and regional booksellers, make friends with the staff. Who arranges the speakers for story time? Is there a children's book specialist? If you present at an author visit to a school, consider asking the bookstore to provide sales. Recently, I spoke at a district that didn't allow the author to bring books to sell. Only later did I learn that the local bookstore could have sold books for me. Make friends with the staff and learn what that bookstore is willing to do!

Educational & Library Distributors. Educational distributors such as Follett, Mackin, Brodart, and more often have insight into what educators or librarians want to buy. Again, meet the staff and offer to cooperate wherever possible. The distributors also have advertising opportunities in catalogs and on their websites. Carefully weigh the costs and the distributor's expertise in your area. But sometimes, these may make sense.

Conventions or conferences. Becoming a speaker on the conference circuit is a viable choice for selling books. Besides expertise in literacy and your topic areas, it helps if you're an entertainer. I've seen conference staff consistently choose a speaker who evokes a laugh, hoping to give the conference participants a good time.

Other Audiences. It's impossible for me to discuss all the ways you can connect with your audience. Would it appeal to chicken farmers, ballerinas, or foster parents? Where do those folks hang out? How can you reach them? You'll need to find creative ways to reach your best audiences and bring them into your marketplace.

What Kind of Presentation?

When you ask kids what kinds of books they want to read, they overwhelmingly vote for humor. Teachers love humor, too. I've attended teacher or library conferences where the author is off in a small room, while the keynote speaker is a comedian. The audience wants entertainment.

Also, give the educators something they can immediately use in their classroom. This might be a discussion guide, coloring page, worksheet, or access to a video interview. The less preparation required of them, the better. They'll be more likely to use it immediately and to repeat using the resource.

As you develop speeches and programs, think about educating your audience, but also about entertaining and inspiring them. Make them laugh and make them weep. And they'll invite you back.

● ● ● ● ● ● ●

ACTION: Research local and regional organizations that are involved in children's literature. If they have a conference, study their call for proposals. Depending on their needs, develop a proposal and send it in. If you're invited to speak, plan carefully and overdeliver! Develop relationships in each organization and keep them updated on new books, awards, or other information.

Chapter 47
Awards

As an indie author, do you submit to book awards? It's one marketing strategy that might be a long shot, but if you win, it could pay off. I often enter my books into book awards. Awards for my independently published books include:

- Four starred PW or Kirkus reviews
- Four NSTA Outstanding Science Trade Books
- Five Eureka! Nonfiction Honor books (CA Reading Assn.)
- Two Junior Library Guild selections
- CLA Notable Children's Book in Language Arts
- Notable Social Studies Trade Book
- Best STEM Book

Why submit?

When you're traditionally published, the publisher must decide which books to submit to which awards. Early in my indie publishing career, I realized that my books probably would NOT have been submitted for awards by a traditional press. Yet—my books received that award. In the legacy world, more established writers would have taken precedence, especially when there are costs or fees per book submitted. As an indie publisher, though, I decide which to submit. And I always err on the side of taking the risk to submit.

First, I think the odds are good. If you want your book to stand out in "today's crowded market," it's hard. These awards, however, have a small number of entries. The recent NSTA Outstanding Science Trade Book award had about 200 children's science books submitted and about 50 were recognized. The odds are much better that you'll be noticed. Submissions to other prizes will vary, but usually the pool of books is smaller than what you'll find in the general market.

Second, I want to publish the best books possible. Someone once said that they didn't want to compete against acclaimed author Mo Willems for awards. Well, I do! I want to compete against the very best of children's books and find a place of excellence for my work. Win or lose, you'll learn something about levels of quality (from that particular set of judges, anyway). And that's helpful for the next books and for your long-term publishing program.

Third, if you win, your marketing gets a boost. It gives you something to talk about, an audience to address, and a long-term reason to talk about the book.

Fourth, if you don't win, you still put your book into the hands of influential readers. The judges may remember the book and use it for a class or read-aloud sometime later. Or, they may recommend it later to friends and colleagues. If you don't have an extensive mailing list for sending advance review copies, award judges are a good place to seed the market.

How to Submit

Each book award looks for certain types of books to honor, so there are a wide variety of choices. As you consider where to send, pay attention to these things: entry fees, membership requirements, criterion for judging, deadlines for submission, and number of books required.

Some awards are too pricey for me. I've seen some require a $75 entry fee, along with ten copies of the book to be given to judges. That's a lot of investment into a single award. For more on contests to avoid, see the ALLI (Alliance of Independent Authors, a British organization for self-published authors) listing of Book Award and Contest Ratings (https://selfpublishingadvice.org/author-awards-contests-rated-reviewed/). Also, be aware that an award by itself won't sell books; however, the recognition is useful in your overall marketing; it may also lead to marketing in a niche market that fits your book.

Where to Submit: Children's Book Awards

This is a list of respected children's book awards. Please research each list carefully and consider entry fee, membership requirements, criterion for judging, deadlines for submission, number of books required, and your own criterion before submitting. Some lists will explicitly say that they are open to indie or self-published books, while others say nothing about that. I always assume that submissions from my publishing house, Mims House, are welcome.

• Aesop Prize and Aesop Accolades (folk tales are classified as nonfiction)
  • Africana Book Awards -- African heritage books
  • Alex Awards - teen awards
  • ALSC Children's Notable Lists
  • Amelia Bloomer List -- feminist books
  • American Indian Youth Literature Award
  • Americas Book Award for Children's and Young Adult Literature (Latin America related books)

• Asian/Pacific American Awards for Literature
• Benjamin Franklin Awards | Independent Book Publisher's Association
• Bologna Ragazzi Awards (International -- through Bologna Children's Book Fair)
• Boston Globe-Horn Book Awards
• Carter G. Woodson Book Awards from National Council for the Social Studies
• Charlotte Zolotow Awards (picture books, ages birth to 7)
• Children's Choice Book Awards (CBC and IRA, child-selected awards)
• Children's Crown Collection (National Christian School Association. Grades 1-8)
• Christopher Awards -- Books that affirm the highest values of the human spirit
• Claudia Lewis Award (Bank Street College; poetry book)
• Coretta Scott King Award
• Cybils -- Sponsored by Book Bloggers
• Eureka! Nonfiction Children's Book Award (California Reading Assn)
• Flora Stieglitz Straus Award (Bank Street College of Education; nonfiction book that serves as an inspiration to young readers)
• Foreword Book of the Year Awards -- Indie Fab
• Giverny Award (science picture book, especially plant science)
• Golden Kite Award (SCBWI) (See also the Spark Award)
• Governor General's Literary Awards (Canada)
• Green Earth Book Award (Newton Marasco Foundation)
• Growing Good Kids, Excellence in Children's Literature Award (American Horticultural Society (gardening and nature topics)
• Gryphon Award for Children's Literature (CBBC; early chapter books for transitional reading)
• Jane Addams Book Award (world peace)
• Judy Lopez Memorial Award - for middle grade titles

• Spark Award (SCBWI) (See also the Golden Kite Award)
• National Outdoor Book Awards
• Norman A Sugarman Children's Biography Award - Cleveland Public Library
• Orbis Pictus Award - nonfiction picture books | NCTE
• Notable Social Studies Trade Books for Young People
• Schneider Family Book Awards (disability related)
• Spur Awards (Western Writers of America)
• Sydney Taylor Honor Book (Association of Jewish Libraries)
• Will Rogers Medallion Award (Originally created to recognize quality works of cowboy poetry that honored the Will Rogers heritage, it has expanded to include other works of Western literature and film.)

• • • • • • •

ACTION: Submit to awards appropriate for your book.

- Look for lists of Children's Book Awards by state.
- Look for lists of local or regional awards.
- Look for lists by genre, keywords, or topic.

Chapter 48
Translations

One common criticism of self-publishing is that you are limited to only a local audience.

Nonsense!

Just like any publisher, you can pursue foreign rights and translations. As I write this, I have my indie books in Chinese (simplified), Portuguese, Spanish, French, Korean, and Catalan. Let's talk about ways to make this happen for your books.

Four Ways Translation Can Happen

I'll start by saying that I only speak English and very bad Spanglish. And poor sign language (which is its own language, too). That means the easy way of translating, that of being bilingual, is not open to me. I must rely on others who are bi-, tri-, or even quad-lingual. Thank you to the translators who help me bring books to kids! Without the translators, I would still only be published in English.

In-Country Interest

Abayomi, the Brazilian Puma is about an orphaned puma cub who lived in an urban area of Brazil. The illustrator, Kitty Harvill, was living in Brazil and wanted to work on a Portuguese translation. She was in contact with puma scientists who were working with schools on wildlife conservation. In Brazil, the publishing process is very different. A government department approves a book project, and then corporations can support the book's expenses in return for conservation credits. I didn't understand the process, but the Brazilians did. Sometimes, the easiest thing to do is find a local person who is interested and motivated to follow that country's publishing process. The result was *Abayomi, um Encontro Feliz*.

For another book, *The Nantucket Sea Monster*, I received an email from a Korean agent who had an interested Korean publisher. I negotiated the contract directly.

Foreign Rights Agency

For Asian rights I've been working with Rightol.cn agency for many years. They are headquartered in Chengdu, China but attend every major book rights festival from the Bologna Children's Festival to the Shanghai Children's Festival. Originally, they contacted me; in fact, I still get occasional inquiries through my website. When contacted, I did a thorough search and vetting process. Rightol is a strong rights agency, representing many U.S. companies. We agreed initially on a two-year contract, because that way I'm not tied to them forever, and vice versa. We agreed that they would only handle Asian rights, their specialty.

They sold a four-book deal to a Chinese company for a term of five years. Unfortunately, that company never produced books. I didn't have to return any money, but I didn't get to see the books. Meanwhile, they sold a six-book Korean deal. The original 4-book deal ran out, and we've now signed a 9-book contract with a different Chinese publisher.

The terms are easy to understand and reasonable. Changes were easily made. What has impressed me about Rightol is that they know how to bargain and haggle over prices. Foreign language deals are never large because the audience for translated books isn't huge in other countries. For most translated books, the market is smaller, so the advances are smaller.

Whatever the first advance is offered, Rightol usually manages to double that before we sign the final contract. In addition, in these Asian contracts, there's a second fee for the digital files. The publishers want and need my original InDesign files (and they do expect InDesign files), and will pay extra for them. That fee is usually double the starting price.

Rightol does charge a percentage of the contract. Chinese, Korean, and other countries expect you to pay taxes on your income, as well. The U.S. does have treaty agreements with some countries that take care of being double taxed, once in China and once in the U.S. Talk to your accountant and lawyer.

So far, this method has earned the most income because I'm paid up front. It's a traditional deal with a legacy publisher for that country, so I earn up front, while they take the risks of publishing the books. It works for me because I don't know how those countries work! Having someone on the ground gives me confidence that the publishing process will be done professionally.

When you look at rights agents, check out their reputation online. If they are good, you'll find lots of deals and recommendations. Pay attention to their territory, if they will represent you worldwide, or only in certain territories. Rightol is great in Asia, but I'd sure like a good agency for worldwide rights. Still looking.

DropCap.com is a rights agency who specializes in working with small and independent publishers. They are strong with adult titles, but are working to develop their children's markets.

Hiring Translators

Because the U.S. has a large population of Spanish-language speakers, I decided to translate five books into Spanish as a test. I hired a Spanish translator that lives in an adjacent state, Mariana Llanos.

Years ago, we hosted an exchange student from France, who is a whiz in languages. She now speaks French, Turkish (her dad was Turkish), English, Spanish, some German, and some Italian. She teaches foreign languages—in other words, she had the credentials to do the French translations. She also translated those five books into French, a riskier translation since the French language market in the U.S. isn't strong. But it was so easy to work with her, our French daughter!

Hiring a translator means you take on all the risk! Just like another book, you produce the translated book, upload to appropriate platforms, and hope it sells enough to earn back your investment.

One strategy is that when you upload to Amazon, instead of choosing Amazon.com as your primary market, you choose an alternate such as Amazon.es (Spain) or Amazon.fr (French). Then, you can run Amazon ads in those languages on the Amazon platform in that country.

If you hire translators, think about marketing. You can hire someone to only translate the book, but you likely want marketing material translated, too. When you upload to Amazon, you have all those spaces to fill up with keywords to help sell the book. Translate those.

After the translation, you can, of course, use translate.google.com, an AI platform such as ChatGPT, or other translation services for updated marketing materials. But it's helpful to get the basic materials translated when the book is translated.

A.I.-Assisted Translation

Scribeshadow is a paid AI-translation service that has grown in popularity recently. Romance authors are translating their whole backlist especially for German, but also Spanish, French, and Italian markets. For romance, the markets are hot! Authors are doubling their income.

But children's books? I'm always skeptical that we can do anything similar to the romance folks. I've listened to their excited chatter, but done nothing.

Scribeshadow is unique because they team up with Problem Solved Translation (PST) services, which means PST offers a human review of the translation. The A.I. program does the heavy lifting—quickly! But you also have a human vet the manuscript, catch colloquialisms, verb tense problems, and generally clean up the A.I.'s work.

Recently, Max from PST posted that some of the translators have a Catalan Project going as an effort to produce more books in that language. There are 10 million speakers of Catalan, and they want a rich variety of books in their language to keep it alive.

I chose *Greatest* for the Catalan test because it is not written in rhyme, which complicates translations, and because it's one of the shortest of my picture books, so the translation fee, which is charged per word, is low. It's also one of my favorite books that I've written!

I emailed Max and asked about children's books. They don't usually do them, but he gave me a price for translating *Greatest* into Catalan, and, hey!—why not? For the Catalan project, they'll be doing promos, perhaps marketing in schools and more. If I jump in now, I'd catch that promo effort of the Catalan Project folks.

For a very reasonable price—well picture books are short, so it can't be very expensive—they provided me the Catalan translation in a week or so. When I uploaded the book to KDP, I chose Amazon.es (Spain) as the main market since the Catalan-speaking area is mostly within Spain.

I'm still conflicted about A.I., but this service, backed up by knowledgeable translators, is likely the way forward in this field. This is a small trial which will allow me to feel my way along.

Will it make money? Who knows? But the risk is very low.

These three ways of getting translated books—agency sales, hiring a translator, or using A.I.-assisted translation with human backup—have allowed me to move forward. I expect the English versions to turn a profit, and taking a small amount of that profit, I'm trying something riskier. It makes good business sense. It's a way to try to expand my reach and develop new sources of income.

· · · · · · ·

ACTION: Decide on how and when you'll search out translations for your book.

Chapter 49
Special Sales

What if...
  ...someone wants to buy your book in bulk and they ask for a discounted price. Will you negotiate a special price? I do.

First, I ask lots of questions about shipping, how they'll use the book, the terms they expect, and so on.

Terms means how will they pay? Typical terms include:

- Credit card payment upon ordering (preferred).
- Net30. Payment is 30 days after receiving your invoice.
- Net90. Payment is 90 days after receiving your invoice.

I always prefer pre-payment with a credit card so there's no question of payment. Sometimes, I'll do a Net30 deal, and I'm very prompt sending the invoice. I don't like longer terms because essentially, I'm giving the customer a short-term loan. Instead, I choose to get my money upfront when possible.

Remember that you're creating a business relationship that you'd like to cultivate. You want them to return over and over for more book purchases. I start with my standard wholesale policy. See the Distribution chapter.

Here's a typical bid request.

BID REQUEST -- Educational Distributor

We'd like to buy 500 copies for use in a curriculum. We need the book in three weeks. What discount do you offer and what's your list price?

For 500 copies, I would probably stick with my wholesale policy of 50% off the SRP. It's not a large enough order to give bigger discounts.

BID REQUEST - Subscription Box Service

We'd like to buy 8000 copies for use in our subscription box. Delivery will be in four months. What discount price can you offer?

Here, the quantity is larger and the delivery time is extended. I would ask U.S. printers for a bid on the book, calculate a percentage profit and give the Box Service a quote based on that. The offset printing is only possible if I have a three or more month lead time. Discounted prices from offset printing in bulk will mean a lower print cost, so I can pass along that savings and still make a profit.

There are no rules here. Some self-publishers flatly refuse to negotiate prices. I tend to negotiate if there is sufficient quantity and enough time to use an offset printer. For smaller quantities, which require POD printing, I will stick with my wholesale policy.

• • • • • • •

ACTION: Decide on your wholesale policy and create a one-page sheet to send when you have inquiries.

Chapter 50
Grassroots

W hen everything fails—or the world shuts down for COVID—it's time to go grassroots. Grassroots marketing means finding your audience and specific ways to communicate directly to them. I briefly covered Grassroots Marketing in the Word of Mouth chapter, but this expands the concept for backlist books.

What was still open?

Erosion is the story of Hugh Bennett, the soil scientist who knew what to do when the Dust Bowl struck the U.S.. He had studied soils for years and worked in Cuba to restore their soil after decades of over-planting sugar cane. I had every expectation that the book would do well. According to the NextGen Science Standards, second graders must study erosion, and the biggest example of that in U.S. history was the Dust Bowl. I was hitting a dual sweet spot of science and social studies in the elementary curriculum. And I was offering up a hero—a soil scientist—who saved the day.

History. Farming. Hero. It should sell well.

But the book launched on June 2, 2020, at the height of the COVID pandemic. With the world shut down, how could I find an audience?

Mims House regularly submits to the teacher awards administered by the Children's Book Council. I submitted *Erosion* to the Notable Social Studies Trade Book and the Outstanding Science Trade Book Award. The science award ignored the book, but the social studies apparently were interested because it's about a major historical event in U.S. history, and Bennett's work resulted in legislation. It was the first time a country passed laws to protect their soil, their natural resources. *Erosion* was named a Notable Social Studies Trade Book award. The award brings a certain amount of recognition as it is promoted among the membership of the National Social Studies Teachers Association.

Next, I researched audiences for children's books about farms. (NOTE: You should really do this sort of research BEFORE you publish a book to establish that there is a readership for the book.) I discovered the National Agriculture in the Classroom organization. The Agriculture in the Classroom is a group of people committed to growing the next generation of farmers. They have a strong network across the U.S., they sponsor events, and they buy books! They invest in the future of farms.

Here's where it goes grassroots.

For each state organization, I found lists of staff members, and looked for those interested in children's books and putting books into the hands of kids. It was a jackpot. I emailed many interested and influential people, with an offer of a review copy (digital, since it was during the COVID pandemic). When they replied, I sent the review copies (because of COVID, they were usually low-resolution pdf files, unless otherwise requested) and an ordering form.

Hugh Bennett set up the U.S. Soil Conservation Service, which has expanded its reach to other natural resources and is now the U.S. Natural Resources Conservation Service, with offices in each state.

Again, I looked up staff and emailed to the appropriate person in each state.

When you do this type of grassroots email, you should manage expectations. Online a 1-3% response rate is great. If you email 100 people and get a response from one to three people, your email campaign was effective.

In this case, I received orders for copies of the book, was invited to do a virtual presentation, and saw the educators spreading the word about the book through their own newsletters. In the depths of the pandemic, I received orders for 250 books, 20 books, or 15 books.

The Agriculture in Education (Ag in Education) movement strongly emphasizes the role of literature in bringing the story of agriculture to students. Along with the Farm Bureaus organization, they select and recommend titles among themselves, and they offer a yearly award, The American Farm Bureau Book of the Year.

They considered *Erosion* for the Farm Bureau Book of the Year award, but I didn't have a strong teacher's guide. The winning book that year did a better job of providing additional resources.

(NOTE TO SELF: If you write on an agriculture topic again, provide a knockout educator's resource packet.)

For grassroots marketing you must identify the person who would buy your book locally, the end user. For *Erosion*, that meant I was looking for educators who would be interested in such a niche topic. And I found them.

Who is your end audience? Where do they hang out? Can you reach them? When you find an audience segment that is highly aligned with your book, and they are easy to contact, it's time for that grassroots marketing effort. Send out dozens or hundreds of emails. I send them one at a time, and try to personalize them when possible. Then, try to respond to those emailing back and answer questions, offer price discounts (when possible), and so on to close a deal.

Grassroots efforts don't always work, but for a targeted audience, it's one of my favorite marketing techniques. To build a grassroots marketing campaign, look for the end users, and then look for ways to contact them. Learn their needs and culture, and create ways for your book and its ancillary materials to meet those needs.

· · · · · · ·

ACTION: Learn about the audience. Do you need to learn more about an organization, maybe take a class with them? Meet with key people? Take someone for coffee?

Research awards. If an organization gives book awards, buy the award-winning book. What kind of teacher materials are available for that book? Notice other details about the award-winning book?

Travel to conference(s). Go to a regional or national conference with the goal of learning more about the needs of this audience. Apply to be a speaker!

Advertise. Are there ways to advertise specifically to this audience?

Part Eight

Educate and Entertain

Entertain and educate. That's what we do.

We write and publish children's books with the purpose of entertaining and/or educating kids. But there are other industries with the same purpose of entertaining and educating: toys and movies. If you capture an audience with publishing, toys, or movies, then you may have opportunities for licensing your characters, plot, story, and so on. You may originate in one industry and license into another. Or, it may be licensing for virtual reality, audio devices, t-shirts, or Halloween costumes. All of these are ways to extend your IP (intellectual property) to products that will bring in revenue.

Because I hold all my copyrights, I can license the characters, plot, story, setting, and so on, whenever I am offered an acceptable contract. But what sorts of contracts are possible? How do you find them? I spent a year exploring adjacent industries to children's book publishing to understand the licensing possibilities for my work. This section is about lifting your eyes from just books to see what else is possible with your intellectual property. We'll look at licensing, toys, and video.

Chapter 51
Licensing

To investigate where my intellectual property might be valuable in adjacent industries, I went to three conferences. My first stop was the Licensing Expo in Las Vegas, the conference where licensing deals of all sorts get made. Movie studios, toy companies, lifestyle companies, and more attend and display. It's a working conference with lots of deals made during the show.

When you register, you have access to the list of attendees and can request a meeting. This is a necessary step because many of the booths are closed to walk-through traffic, only available when you have an appointment. I didn't know this, so I tried to walk into the Paramount booth to see a huge T-Rex Lego creation. Security guards made sure I kept walking.

What kinds of deals could be made here?

There are many categories of deals: T-shirts, kids' clothing, kids' lifestyle (bedding, house decorations, mobiles, rocking chairs, strollers, Halloween costumes, shoes, pencils, and much, much more), puzzles, games, and toys. A growing category is pet toys and products, as people focus on their pets as family. Think Frisbees for dogs.

Deals here are positioned for the widest distribution in stores such as Walmart, Target, TJ Maxx, and so on. International deals are also hot at the Licensing Expo.

When you register, you gain access to the system of setting up conferences. You can request a meeting with any company. Depending on your product proposal, they'll either agree to meet or not. This means the quality of your listing and your proposal matter. Going once helps you understand what is possible in licensing. Consider your first year a learning experience and plan for the next year.

Pitch Decks

At the Expo, pitch decks (PowerPoint presentations) were the most popular way of explaining your product and the opportunities you offer. Everyone carried a laptop and could flip it open to talk about their company and their ideas.

One virtual reality company contacted me about using some books on their product. Many companies have great technology ideas of how to bring stories and content to kids. The problem? Content. They concentrate on the technology and perfect it, but they don't have the library of content to back it up. What good is XYZ technology, if you don't have multiple stories for kids to listen to or watch? That means opportunities for indie publishers, and it's exciting to see the new opportunities. This deal fell through for strange reasons, but it's an example of what you can do when just starting out.

WIT - Women in Toys

(Sorry men, skip this paragraph.) One recommended organization is Women in Toys, an organization devoted to helping women succeed in the business of toys. At the Licensing Expo, they provided a break room in the Michael Jackson Theater Lounge. They served a lunch of cold cuts and had snacks throughout the day. Stepping into the room, you felt the energy of the women and, especially, the encouragement. It was a great first introduction to this organization, which will feature larger in the report from the Toy Fair. Here, it's important to say that they were there, and they were supportive.

Future Conventions

I had few meetings this first year, but mostly walked around and got a feel for what's possible. To display, a booth is very expensive, which means that if I return, I'll focus on setting up meetings. Most of the deals are made by big brands for a wide range of products. But sometimes there are smaller deals that help launch a line of products.

Also of interest is the License This! competition, which looks for creative concepts that have potential across multiple lines. I later met someone who had placed in this competition and quickly acquired an agent for her product. It's definitely a way in.

• • • • • • •

ACTION: Evaluate your book's potential for licensing. Usually, licensors will look for proven sales numbers, interesting characters, the visual assets available, and so on. As you create your book, think about the possibilities for t-shirts, toothpaste, and so on. This is an advanced market, so you'll likely need a couple years of sales under your belt before you go to Licensing Expo. Meanwhile, pay attention to licensing deals and dream big!

Chapter 52
Toys

The next industry that also works to entertain and educate kids is the toy market. In 2022, the Women in Toys organization, which works to help women succeed in the toy industry, held a Walmart WIT Empowerment Day in conjunction with the Toy Market in Dallas. This is a marketplace for toy shops to come and view what's new in the marketplace, a time to make deals and place orders.

The Market opened on a Tuesday, so the Empowerment Day took place on Monday. Empowerment Day is set up to allow women creators an opportunity to pitch ideas to industry leaders, directly to the toy companies who produce toys. Mentors were available to answer questions on everything from copyright, to designing a toy prototype, to marketing toys. WIT was awesome in many ways!

Before Empowerment Day, they provided a series of videos and live Zooms setting up expectations and answering questions. The pitches were expected to be sizzle reels, a 1-2 minute video that showed the idea in action. Preferred were videos showing kids actually playing with toys. They also encouraged mocking up photos of how your packaged toy would look on a Walmart store shelf. Yes, I needed a prototype, packaging and more!

My book, *A Little Bit of Dinosaur*, had been read 1,175,000 times on the EPIC! App, the premiere reading app in U.S. schools, with a presence in about 90% of schools. Forbes magazine reported that in 2020,[1] there were one billion reads on the app. My story had over a million in its first year. With an audience of over a million readers in a single year, would I get any attention at the Toy Market or Empowerment Day?

Empowerment Day

I worked hard to get ready for the Empowerment Day, creating one-page sell sheets and a sizzle reel. I knew that I had one big disadvantage: no prototype. In all the prep materials, they emphasized that toy companies wanted to see the toy in action with kids. What I had was a book and an audience.

I didn't plan to produce a prototype. I know publishing, how to commission great art and how to produce a great book. I know how to search for and find readers. But I didn't know the toy industry. Because I knew so little about toys, any prototype I tried would recreate all of the worst of the newbie mistakes. Instead, I hoped to find someone who would find the book and audience combination interesting enough to work with me on creating toys and licensing the work. I knew that was bucking the accepted wisdom, but I also knew that I was unique, coming from the publishing world.

The Empowerment Day was set up well. Communications before were timely and appropriate. I learned that I had pitch sessions with four toy companies and one agency who screened for toy companies. In addition, I could visit any of the mentor tables that I wished.

Pipes framed up a maze of curtained areas for private pitches. At your scheduled time, you were led to an interview area that included a table and chairs. Usually, you had five minutes to set up your computer for your sizzle reel, and any other materials, such as the prototype.

My first session with the agency ended quickly because I didn't have a prototype. They could do nothing, they said, without that. However, I should go to the mentor tables and talk to a person who headed a licensing agency for toys. That conversation went well. An experienced executive, she was intrigued with the story, while puzzled that I didn't have a prototype.

Mentor Tables

Besides the pitches, industry experts chaired a variety of tables. I sat at the publishing table long enough to learn they were explaining traditional publishing. At a product development table, the designer was fascinated with my story and asked me specifically to follow up with her company. Another toy rep was fascinated with the ideas and characters from my story and started throwing out ideas on where else it might go. A marketing executive talked about the importance of child privacy as you develop TikTok marketing videos. There are limits to how long a child can be on screen without an adult, which affects the type of videos possible. Finally, a marketing company talked about new business ideas for e-commerce. All were fascinating and helpful.

The Empowerment Day was amazing, kudos to the WIT organization. The access and education were amazingly appropriate and generous.

The Toy Association Preview and Holiday Market

The next day, I attended the actual Preview and Holiday Market, a huge trade show where toy stores come to place orders. Like the Licensing Expo, there were also opportunities to sign up to pitch ideas behind closed doors. I did none of that because Empowerment

Day gave me so much access. Instead, I walked the floors looking at the new toys.

The exhibition floor was huge (though someone said I should go to the New York City Toy Market to really see a big one). I spent a morning wandering around. I skipped the construction toys section, focusing more on arts & crafts, plush toys, and clothing or lifestyle related sections. Overall, the toys were exciting and colorful. I thought several times about how a book would display next to a toy and which would win a kid's attention.

How Do Kids Play?

One of the more useful takeaways from this year of exploring adjacent industries was to think about Play Patterns. That is, how do kids take an idea, a toy, or ideas from a movie and extend their play? How do they play? We don't think about that because, for us, kids are just reading. They read. They finish the book. Done.

But the other industries have products or series or other ways to keep the kids interacting with their stories and characters. How do they do that?

So, how do kids play: hair play, clothes play, cooking play, baby doll play, outdoor play, action figure play, creative play, imaginary play, storytelling play, racing play, nurturing play, construction play, arts and crafts play, sports play, friend play, and so on.

One example is Pokémon, which is collecting, storytelling, and battling play. That collecting play is massive, making Pokémon one of the highest-grossing games/IP properties ever.

Or think of Paw Patrol, which is about pets and rescue, and has become a pop culture phenomenon. There's transportation, vehicle, storytelling, play set, and transformation. Barbie, on the other extreme, is hair play, fashion play, transformation, and storytelling.

It made me think about my characters and stories in a slightly different way. Am I building into the story the opportunities for kids to play? Could they do storytelling with my characters? Thinking about Play Patterns has the potential to change my approach to story-telling.

• • • • • • •

ACTION: If you're interested in toys related to your books, build play patterns into the story line. Study the type of toy that interests you and consider creating and refining prototypes. Then investigate the best toy companies for your toy/book and read their submission guidelines. Again, have fun!

Chapter 53
Video

K ids books do find their way to the screen, such as Doreen Cronin's short chapter series *Chicken Squad*, which inspired an animated series that debuted on Disney Junior in May 2021.[1]

My exploration of kids movies and videos started with a podcast with Joanna Penn interviewing Chrissy Metge, a movie industry professional.[2] Chrissy was offering to review pitches for Kidscreen Summit, the annual conference of people interested in video for kids.

Kidscreen is an expensive conference, but in 2023, they still had a virtual conference, which was more reasonable and didn't include travel. I registered early enough that I could sign up for pitches.

A pitch, like in publishing, is when you present an idea to a person acquiring for their company. I was lucky enough to draw pitches to Peacock Streaming, Disney Junior, and Sesame Street. Fortunately, I had Chrissy's help in preparing a pitch deck (a targeted PowerPoint presentation) about my Kittytubers series, and the sessions went well. No one was interested in my ideas, but the process was fascinating to see how publishing does and doesn't dovetail with kids movies.

The movie industry terminology is different from publishers. They prefer a sizzle reel (1–2 minute video) that hypes your story, rather than the pitch deck. They want to see and hear the concept instead of just read about it. But otherwise, they are just looking for that fresh idea that will stand out in today's crowded market!

They also have a full schedule. I was pitching my Kittytubers chapter book series, and I heard again and again that they had cat characters already. Mine was vastly different, but it didn't matter. Cats are cats, in their opinion. Another rejection noted that I had the wrong audience age range. Disney Junior focuses on the preschool audience, and my story was for an older group. Peacock Streaming was specifically looking for properties to appeal to girls—but they already had cats. Each company had specific needs, and my work didn't fill those needs.

Interesting also was the expectation that you would participate in fund-raising. One minute of animation can cost $5,000 to $50,000+. For high-end films, it can go very high. They always wanted to know if there were funding possibilities.

Networking

A final advantage of attending such a conference was networking. I virtually met several people, including an IP attorney. A great lawyer is crucial when you start moving outside the publishing industry. Actually, I think they are important for us, too. I've used lawyers to create a boilerplate contract for audiobook narrators and illustrators and think this is of vital importance. If my publishing contracts aren't right, I won't be able to step out into other areas either. The lawyer I had used initially retired, and I wasn't particularly happy with her suggested replacements.

At Kidscreen, a certain lawyer moderated one session, and I liked her approach to things. I sent her a connection invitation on LinkedIn and met with her the next month when I attended a writing conference in her area. Her wide experience and her enthusiasm convinced me to work with her for future contracts.

• • • • • • •

ACTION: Study the kids video market to see how your book might adapt to video. Investigate video companies who create kids entertainment, looking for a connection to your stories. Consider going to Kidscreen to learn more and to pitch your ideas.

Part Nine
Moving Forward

As you move forward in your writing and publishing journey, I have a last word of encouragement for you!

Chapter 54
Your Publishing Legacy

In twenty years, will kids remember any of your books? 100 years? Dr. Seuss died over thirty years ago, yet *The Cat in the Hat* is still popular with elementary school readers. He's known for a handful of titles among the over sixty books he authored.

Will any of your books rise to that level?

You've learned much about yourself over the course of this book. You learned what motivates you strongly to write, your passions and interests. You've learned how to be courageous and persistent, to never give up but to face failures with hope and endurance. You've learned to solve hard problems, and still smile at the dawning of a new day. That courage, that joy in life will come out in your writing. You will connect with readers.

But your journey as a creative writer and publisher isn't done. You can actively control your legacy.

Grow. Your writing will change and develop. Let it mature. Follow your ideas and your heart to create books that you are passionate about. It's fine to change to new publishing areas, as long as you realize it could affect your success in the short term.

Persevere. Remember that Patience chapter at the beginning?

This is the mature phase of patience. We wait for things to happen, and when you've waited for many, many things to happen, you have persevered.

Adapt. Life throws us curves. When I had to have a knee-replacement surgery, I planned ahead to finish writing, to sign contracts with illustrators who would keep working while I recovered, and to schedule blog posts and such. Fortunately, I had warning and took the time to plan for several weeks off and several more weeks of reduced hours.

When life throws you a surprise curve, adapt. As a solo entrepreneur, life can take a toll on your business. Be kind to yourself, and just do what you can, when you can.

Write. Keep writing. I am a publisher second, a writer first. Everything I do depends on regularly putting words on paper. Write, write, write, Publish.

Connect. Finally, remember: Writing + Reader = Success

Your success depends on finding and connecting with your reader.

Find ways to keep writing and publishing.

Find ways to build Word of Mouth.

Find ways to connect with your readers.

Happy writing! Happy publishing!

Checklist

Notes

5. Respect Your Own Opinion

1. https://www.slj.com/review/nefertiti-the-spidernaut-the-jumping-spider-who-learned-to-hunt-in-space
2. The Gifts of Tony Sarg: American Experience | PBS. https://www.pbs.org/video/gifts-tony-sarg-american-experience-pbs/

10. The Alpha Generation

1. Tuchów, Ryan. Kids Shifting from YouTube to TikTok at Age 10. Kidscreen website. https://kidscreen.com/2022/09/12/kids-shifting-from-youtube-to-tiktok-at-age-10/ September 12, 2022.
2. Newton, Derek. Reading Platform Epic Had an Epic Year. Forbes Magazine online. https://www.forbes.com/sites/dereknewton/2021/01/25/reading-platform-epic-had-an-epic-year/ January 25, 2021.

12. Copyright: The Super-Power of Self-Publishing

1. Smith, Dean Wesley. Killing the Top Ten Sacred Cows of Publishing: #8...You Can't Make a Living With Your Fiction. Dean Wesley Smith: Opinions and Writings website. https://deanwesleysmith.com/killing-the-top-ten-sacred-cows-of-publishing-8-you-cant-make-a-living-with-your-fiction/ December 17, 2013

13. Multiple Roles

1. For more on copyright see this blog post.
   Pattison, Darcy. Copyright is Our Business. Indie Kids Books blog. https://www.indiekidsbooks.com/p/copyright-is-our-business July 14, 2022.
2. Here's a good tutorial on setting up your business.
   Chesson, Dave. How to Start a Publishing Company in 2025 (Legal + Strategy). Kindlepreneur website. https://kindlepreneur.com/how-to-start-a-publishing-company/. January 23, 2025.

Notes

30. Distribution

1. Friedman, Jane. The Challenge of Driving Demand for Books: Interview with Peter Hildick-Smith. JaneFriedman.com April 5, 2005. (Paywall) https://jane-friedman.com/the-challenge-of-driving-demand-for-books-interview-with-peter-hildick-smith/
2. Penguin Random House. How to Order blog post. https://penguinrandomhouse elementaryeducation.com/2019/10/21/how-to-order/ October 21, 2019

31. Metadata

1. Nielsen Book: The Importance of Metadata for Discoverability and Sales. https://nielsenbook.co.uk/wp-content/uploads/2022/04/Nielsen-Metadata-Marketing-Report.pdf c. 2021 The Nielsen Company.

32. Fan-Loyalty

1. Friedman, Jane. The Challenge of Driving Demand for Books: Interview with Peter Hildick-Smith. (Paywall) https://janefriedman.com/the-challenge-of-driving-demand-for-books-interview-with-peter-hildick-smith/
2. Superawesome. Alpha Impact: How Kids Are Shaping Media, Tech & Commerce report. 2025. https://www.superawesome.com/alpha-impact-how-kids-are-shaping-media-tech-commerce/

52. Toys

1. Newton, Derek. Reading Platform Epic Had An Epic Year. Forbes Magazine online. January 25, 2021. https://www.forbes.com/sites/dereknewton/2021/01/25/reading-platform-epic-had-an-epic-year/

53. Video

1. Lodge, Sally. TV Alert: Disney Junior to Adapt 'The Chicken Squad'. Publisher's Weekly online. May 4, 2021.
   https://www.publishersweekly.com/pw/by-topic/childrens/childrens-industry-news/article/86242-tv-alert-disney-junior-to-adapt-the-chicken-squad.html
2. Penn, Joanna. Pitching A Book For Film Or TV With Chrissy Metge. November 8, 2021. The Creative Penn Podcast. https://www.thecreativepenn.com/2021/11/08/pitching-a-book-for-film-or-tv-with-chrissy-metge/

Acknowledgments

I want to thank these children's book authors who gave me early feedback on this book: Rinda Beach, Azizi Birkeland, Laura Pepper, Nicole Loy, and Sandra Acharya. And thanks to my husband, Dwight, for giving me the space and encouragement to pursue my passion of children's books.

About the Author

Children's book author and indie publisher Darcy Pattison writes award-winning fiction and non-fiction books for children. Her works have received starred PW, Kirkus, and BCCB reviews. Awards include the Irma Black Honor award, five NSTA Outstanding Science Trade Books, six Eureka! Nonfiction Honor book, two Junior Library Guild selections, two NCTE Notable Children's Book in Language Arts, a Notable Social Studies Trade Books, a NSTA Best STEM book, and an Arkansiana Award. She's the 2007 recipient of the Arkansas Governor's Arts Award for Individual Artist for her work in children's literature. Her works are translated into eleven languages.

Always active, before her tenth birthday, she (almost) climbed the Continental Divide, turning back at the last twenty yards because it was too steep and great climbing shoes hadn't been invented yet. She once rode a bicycle down a volcano in Bali, Indonesia and has often hiked the Rockies. She's hiked New Zealand's backcountry for a taste of Kiwi life, and then strolled the beaches of Australia. In 2024, she (finally) climbed the 14,043 foot Mt. Sherman in Colorado—hurrah for great hiking shoes. On her bucket list is kayaking the Nā Pali Coast of Hawaii and eating curry in Mumbai.

For Darcy's books, see MimsHouseBooks.com